Diagnosis
and
the difference
it makes

Diagnosis
and
the difference
it makes

EDITED BY PAUL W. PRUYSER

Jason Aronson, Inc.
New York

TABLE OF CONTENTS

Diagnosis
and
the difference
it makes

INTRODUCTION

PAUL W. PRUYSER, Ph.D.*

With a conference on "Diagnosis and the Difference It Makes" the Menninger Foundation celebrated in 1975 its fiftieth anniversary. Why was this topic chosen? Today, can anyone think of a more hackneyed psychiatric subject than diagnosis? In the 1970s, are not many psychiatrists disenchanted with diagnostic issues, their patients disgruntled over psychiatric labels, and the general public puzzled and disheartened with the plethora of diagnostic categories and the lack of psychiatric agreement about their meaning or significance? In fact, is it not a widespread belief that even if a diagnosis is made, it does not seem to make much of a difference except for the social backlash attached to some ill-conceived diagnostic designations?

At first blush, such negative or nihilistic reactions to psychiatric diagnosis seem to be quite apropos, given the atmosphere of malcontent with diagnosis that prevails even within the professional circle of psychiatry, including the governing boards and committees of psychiatry's professional organizations. But a closer look may show that what is apropos is not always warranted. Being malcontent with diagnosis, if it leads merely to negativism or nihilism, does not constitute adequate reality testing. The fact is that at the present time—no less than in psychiatry's history—diagnostic thought in one way or another is the profession's central activity and

---

* Henry March Pfeiffer Professor, The Menninger Foundation, Topeka, Kansas. Dr. Pruyser served as chairman of the conference, "Diagnosis and the Difference It Makes," and has acted as consulting editor to this expanded issue of the *Bulletin of the Menninger Clinic*.

the organizing principle of most of its textbooks and institutions. Though forever caught in the flow of changing concepts and just as controversial today as it was during the careers of the humanitarian Pinel, the antinosological Neumann, the pragmatic Esquirol, and the metaphysical Heinroth, diagnosis is still the Copernican point of psychiatric thought and activity. Psychiatric thought indeed carries enormous historical baggage; but if anyone simply seeks to divest himself of its unexamined bulk, the dangerous ignorance of such an act of bravado would doom him to repeating all the errors of the past.

Whether one likes it or not and regardless of its particular form at any given time, diagnosis is a powerful definer of psychiatric patienthood. But equally powerful and more disastrous is the benign (or slothful) neglect that refuses the right of patienthood to anyone, leaving it to the *vox populi* to decry whomever it wishes as "crazy," "nuts," or "kooky," thus dispatching them to limbo.

Diagnosis transcends local and national boundaries; despite all the cultural differences, diagnosis is a worldwide preoccupation and diagnostic results form the basis of any plan anywhere for rendering mental health services, as well as for their dissemination and improvement. Psychiatric diagnosis is what third parties, such as governments and private insurance companies, pay for. Psychiatric diagnosis is what the courts and penal and eleemosynary institutions want to be apprised of and for which they make fiscal allocations.

Diagnosis is what psychiatric patients expect to receive, and rightfully so. Although patients and prospective patients may, for good or bad reasons, protest against diagnostic procedures and formulations, they are certainly entitled to the most thorough and sophisticated assessment of their predicaments and conditions. If one were to argue that the ideal psychiatric diagnosis is a product of the patient's own self-searching with the help of one or more professional resource persons who specialize in dealing with mental woes, that it is in effect a self-assessment, one would be saying that diagnosis is no trivial matter. That kind of diagnosing is a supreme act of human freedom and existential obligation.

Diagnosis is what precedes, or should precede, all other psychiatric activities. If, in melioristic zeal, one prefers to emphasize treatment over diagnosis with all the semantic trapeze work that this noble sounding preference entails, one would be actually less reasonable to allow diagnostic thought to be absorbed into therapeutic work than to engage in diagnostic work with therapeutic thought and intention. For while it is true in a dialectical sense that diagnosis and treatment cry out for each other, the ordinary march of time that organizes actual work makes diagnosis the necessary precursor to any judiciously chosen treatment modality.

In one sense, then, diagnosis is and has always been the most elementary psychiatric act, for the diagnostician as well as the patient. In another sense, it is the ultimate psychiatric process requiring the most advanced knowledge and skill and demanding the greatest wisdom on both sides of the diagnostic relationship.

During the Menninger Foundation's first fifty years, 1925 to 1975, diagnostic work has been assiduously pursued and has received the most thoughtful attention, both conceptually and operationally. Almost from the start, diagnostic work led to research, induced the formation of the multidisciplinary psychiatric team, and formed the backbone of educational training programs for the various mental health professions. Diagnostic observations laid the groundwork for preventive activities and led boldly from dealing with patients to addressing nonclinical persons, groups, and situations. Far from its being done impassively, with a feeling of contentment about the prevailing views, techniques, and vocabulary that reigned in the professions, the Menninger Foundation's diagnostic work was led by a critical, reformative spirit. Karl and Will Menninger and their colleagues were restive regarding the state of diagnostic thought and practice during their careers. They found much to criticize in the mentality, attitudes, habits, word usage, and apparent goallessness that beset the diagnostic atmosphere of their time. They sought an entirely new "grammar" of diagnosing and shared their revisionist views with colleagues as well as the public.

Their work is not finished. They themselves never regarded it so. The topic of psychiatric diagnosis is virtually inexhaustible—diagnosis is the topic that runs through all of psychiatric history, forever redefining psychiatric practices as well as the outlook of people in general on mental disorder. What counts is constant modernization of the processes and concepts and goals of diagnosing. What counts is the courage to take distance from one's own professional habits so as to see clearly their premises and outcomes. What counts is willingness to realign one's diagnostic practices with perennial humanitarian and scientific ideals as well as the new exigencies that reality forever seems to impose.

In 1930, Karl Menninger wrote the following opening paragraphs to his best-selling book *The Human Mind*:

> When a trout rising to a fly gets hooked on a line and finds itself unable to swim about freely, it begins a fight which results in struggles and splashes and sometimes an escape. Often, of course, the situation is too tough for him.
>
> In the same way the human being struggles with his environment and with the hooks that catch him. Sometimes he masters his difficulties; sometimes they are too much for him. His struggles are all that the world sees and it usually misunderstands them. It is hard for a free fish to understand what is happening to a hooked one.
>
> Sooner or later, however, most of us get hooked. How much of a fight we have on our hands then depends on the hook, and, of course, on us. If the struggle gets too violent, if it throws us out of the water, if we run afoul of other strugglers, we become 'cases' in need of help and understanding [p. 3].

Almost half a century later, mental health practitioners should be attuned to the same ideal of compassionate understanding even though faced with clinical and social questions of larger scope: What if the "trout" is a family rather than an individual? What if the "struggling fish" is a small group, a large group, an organization, a community, a social institution? What, indeed, if the "hooked fish" is a whole culture? If all of these become "cases in need of help and understanding"—as they seem to be doing so glaringly in the 1970s— can psychiatric assessment of them provide the necessary understanding and devise appropriate and workable forms of help? What are the next evolutions of psychiatric diagnosis and what are the differences in human well-being they can make?

These questions are altogether a large order for the human mind and may overtax one's ingenuity. But they are not spurious questions. That they sound somewhat desperate only testifies to their relevance and actuality. The papers that follow are attempts to come to grips with these questions, one by one, cautiously or boldly, according to each author's outlook and temperament.

Setting the stage for a discourse on diagnosis is the opening section entitled "Critique and Adequacy of Psychiatric Diagnosis." Pruyser and Menninger analyze the language of diagnosis, with its diverse origins in nosology, classification, and therapeutics, arguing that an unpresumptuous "person language" in the mother tongue is needed to define human predicaments. Then Shectman examines in dialogue form the pros and cons of diagnosing, taking up one by one the objections to diagnosis that have been voiced by various contemporary critics.

In the second section, "Action, the Diagnostic Focus," Schafer gives direction to the diagnostic process as well as its content by selecting action as the nub of experience, pathology, diagnosis, and therapy, and by presenting a grand review and reinterpretation of Freud's (1926) "Inhibitions, Symptoms and Anxiety" under the telling title "Danger Situations."

The authors of the papers included in the third section, "The Varying Scopes of Psychiatric Diagnosis," tackle the question: Who or what are the various diagnostic "subjects"? De la Torre, Appelbaum, Chediak, and Smith begin with the traditional individual psychiatric patient as a solid and solitary diagnostic subject. Mandelbaum moves from the designated patient to the family, considering it a more appropriate unit for diagnostic evaluation. Horwitz and Colson each present papers in which they focus on therapeutic groups. Brocher then examines how organizations can be diagnosed —not only how their healthy and unhealthy internal processes can be understood but also what impact they have on organizational members. In the last article in the section, Roy Menninger investigates whether society and culture can be appraised diagnostically and includes a discussion of those professions set apart within society to do the diagnosing.

The papers included in the fourth section are directed toward a different set of questions: From what vantage points do specific professions or disciplines attempt to give diagnosis maximal relevance and pertinence? Ayd, identified with psychopharmacology, finds this special knowledge base a guide to diagnostic observations and inferences. Modlin, well-known in forensic psychiatry, exposes the "in-house" troubles with diagnosis that psychiatry has experienced in trying to buttress the psychiatrist in his role as expert witness. Appelbaum and Smith, two clinical psychologists, each present papers in which they take psychological testing as their frame of reference and find in its unique data base and inference process a special perspective on diagnosis. Finally, we hear representatives of two disciplines which, while highly relevant to psychiatry and sharing many concepts and practices with it, are rooted in altogether different professional traditions and derive from nonmedical and nonpsychiatric basic sciences which have their own autonomy. Hiltner, a pioneer in modern pastoral education, discusses the contributions of the theological disciplines and traditions to diagnostic assessment. Briar, dean of a school of social work, seeks to define a specific social perspective in diagnostic work by examining social theory and social policy.

A brief epilogue puts all diagnostic work, however approached and conceived, in the service of caring.

References

FREUD, SIGMUND (1926): Inhibitions, Symptoms and Anxiety. *Standard Edition* 20:77–175, 1959.

MENNINGER, K. A: *The Human Mind.* New York: Knopf, 1930.

Critique and Advocacy
of Psychiatric Diagnosis

LANGUAGE PITFALLS IN DIAGNOSTIC THOUGHT AND WORK

PAUL W. PRUYSER, Ph.D.*
KARL MENNINGER, M.D.†

Introduction

Long, long ago, a seriously disturbed person said of himself, "My name is Legion." Being possessed by multiple devils, his cure involved no less than a whole herd of swine who ran away with his ills, stampeded to their death, and left him behind in sober and sane simplicity. Legion have been the psychiatric patients in the history of mankind; legion also have been the names of their illnesses. Seventy pages of fine print in the appendix to *The Vital Balance* (Menninger *et al.* 1963) record the ever-changing list of these names, swelling and shrinking in number over the ages, alternating between sacred and vernacular designations, cheapening from scientific terms to household words, and sometimes regressing from clear descriptions to obfuscating prestige terms, in an astonishing juggler's act with language.

Today, Legion is no longer the name of the patients and their disorders. Despite the comeback of popular demonology and exor-

---

* Henry March Pfeiffer Professor, The Menninger Foundation, Topeka, Kansas.
† Chairman, Board of Trustees, The Menninger Foundation, Topeka, Kansas.

cism, the name has fallen into disuse. We propose, however, that the name Legion may be an apt designation of today's professional psychiatrist, alerting us to the fact that psychiatry is a multilingual enterprise. In this profession, expertise in word usage is of the utmost importance. Psychiatric work entails engagement in several distinct language games, each with its own syntax, grammar, and vocabulary. It also entails the responsibility of keeping these languages apart, differentiating them from each other, and using each one appropriately, commensurate with the purpose at hand.

Since one metaphor may easily lead to another by a process of associative drift, let us warn you that by the name *Legion* we are not alluding to the confusion of tongues alleged to exist *among* psychiatrists. We are not trying to describe the house of psychiatry as a Tower of Babel, whose workers stalled the enterprise of reaching to the sky because they could not communicate with each other. Our focus is on the confusion of tongues existing *within* each psychiatrist, on account of which he fails to have conceptual order and clarity of meanings within himself. We name him Legion in the sense that the course of his work, and its various contexts, force him to speak a multitude of languages which he often has difficulty in keeping apart. In a day's routine, the psychiatrist converses with a patient, consoles a distraught relative, jots down technical notes to himself, and composes reports for others to read. He hears reports from nurses, psychologists, social workers, and others. He reads laboratory data, conducts purposeful interviews, and makes telephone calls. He writes letters to judges, lawyers, and insurance companies. He fills out government forms, dictates process notes about his therapeutic work, uses the *Diagnostic and Statistical Manual of Mental Disorders* (DSM-II), receives consultations, and presumably goes home for dinner to engage with his family. All these activities and situations involve language—spoken, heard, written, or read—and that language is not one unitary system such as basic English or Esperanto. On the contrary, the psychiatrist speaks, hears, writes, and reads in a multiplicity of tongues, dialects, cants, argots, arcana, vernaculars, quasi-sacred phrases, languages of fact, conviction, or common sense, and at times abracadabra. To survey and comment on these various languages of the psychiatrist is the purpose of this presentation.

The Languages of a Psychiatrist

What languages do we hear our man Legion speak? What language should he speak, or what languages might he learn to speak properly if he is to be a well-versed polyglot rather than a babbling Legion?

When one ponders these questions, several large language groupings come to mind. Psychiatry has long known four distinct language games: the language of nosology, the language of classification, the language of persons, and the language of therapeutic techniques. To be sure, the first two of these are often confused, so we will shortly set forth the differences. It is tempting to recognize from the start also a language of diagnosis, but we should withstand that temptation because diagnostic word usage is in fact most often an amalgam of the other four languages—a kind of supralanguage of the greatest artificiality. Anticipating some distinctions we shall make, we may say now that diagnostic language looms as the most problematic of all psychiatric languages, as the most haphazard linguistic artifact of the profession, as the most widely abused conflation of words, and the most manneristic form of psychiatric speech making. Let us first survey the four basic languages.

The Language of Nosology

Though often taken to be identical, nosology and classification are not the same thing. A system of classification is an exercise in taxonomy, guided by rules or laws of grouping. The DSM-II is such a system. Nosology is the conceptualization of disease, yielding the material or entities that are subsequently to be grouped. For instance, Bleuler's text (1911) on the schizophrenias is a nosological work, not a classification.

Nosological language is a symbol system in the service of the science that treats of diseases. Nosologists want to know what a disease is, and they regard any particular disease within the context of some conceptual definition of disease in general. The relation between the general and the particular raises profound nosological questions, differently posed and answered in different epochs of psychiatric history. For instance, when the general theory of humors prevailed, particular diseases of humoral nature were formulated, e.g., Galen's melancholia. When fevers assumed cardinal importance, particular mental disorders became differentiated in terms of presence or absence of fever, e.g., Hippocrates's phrenitis versus mania, and some deliriums of later writers. Prominence of sexual pathology in the general theory led to the formulation of such specific diseases as hysteria, satyriasis, the incubus of the Middle Ages and Renaissance, the dysphrenia sexualis of Kahlbaum, and the various degeneracy conditions described as neurasthenia and psychasthenia. When it was believed that all mental disorder was brain disease (e.g., Griesinger), the various clinical pictures were seen as phases of one organic process or as distinguishable reaction types.

Thus, nosological ideas tend to derive from two very different sets of historical determinants. The first set is composed of high-level conceptions of disease in general which range from philosophical to empirical. They are saddled with a heritage that includes on the one hand moral, religious, mythological, and demonological speculations; on the other hand, anatomical, endocrinological, neurological, psychological, or social extrapolations. The second set consists of lower-level descriptions of distinguishable clinical conditions or courses of illness, amounting to word pictures saddled with a heritage of folklore (hysteria, lycanthropy), arcana (hypochondriasis), names of people (Korsakoff syndrome), age-specific descriptions (adjustment reaction of adolescence, senile dementia, dementia praecox), and a large array of terms derived from presumed specific agents (alcoholism), specific emotions (depression, mania), specific habits (certain behavior disturbances in children), specific developmental arrests (mental deficiency), specific character structures (infantile personality), or specific social nuisances (psychopathic personalities).

More often than not, nosologists have tried to keep the old words current while changing their general or particular meanings by offering definitions of their own. Some brave souls, such as Adolf Meyer, seeing the pitfalls of the inherited nomenclature, tried to invent new words for subgroups of the clinical pictures they wished to distinguish (e.g., parergasia, thymergasia) and added words to denote their general conception of mental disorder (e.g., considering all of them reaction types). As a result, nosological language is full of archaisms, representing a plethora of hand-me-down words ill-suited to foster either a generic understanding of mental disorder or a clear grasp of any specific condition.

The Language of Classification

The language of classification is thoroughly confused by ambiguities about its use and application. The first noteworthy ambiguity pertains to what is to be classified, disorders or patients? Though the DSM-II purports to be an aid in the classification of disorders, its users frequently subvert it to a scheme for organizing patient statistics. Some patients have more than one disorder and would thus require multiple allocations to the entries in the classification system. Moreover, there is no generic rule, other than arbitrary, for ranking these patients' several disorders in terms of primary, secondary, tertiary, or subsequent orders of importance. Particularly when diagnoses are made to establish viable interventions, the therapeutic emphasis may be on a secondary or tertiary condition or symptom rather than the primary one.

A second important ambiguity in the language of psychiatric classification is due to the tension that exists between the conceptual generality of nosology and the clinical specificity of the individual case. A taxonomic system requires recognized constants that define each class at specified levels of abstraction. Though few scientific classification systems of complex entities have reached the degree of perfection of which the chemist's periodic table is the showcase, the entities of psychiatric taxonomy are notorious for their descriptive imprecision, and the scope of this taxonomy is notorious for the latitude granted to it in different eras. Galen recognized only a handful of disorders; Boissier de Sauvages formulated a dozen classes and hundreds of genera; and Neumann settled for only one disorder, to be called "insanity." Admittedly, psychiatry deals with many variables; therefore its classification schemes are more unwieldy than those of other disciplines which deal with fewer variables. But in all sciences the variables that count are abstracted from hordes of candidates most of which are rejected by a careful screening process. Obviously psychiatry has not yet been able to sort out the viable from the unproductive variables, and therefore its classification systems are beset by inconsistencies.

Thirdly, in psychiatry, no two cases of the alleged same disorder are alike to a firmly acceptable degree. Nor are the variables that differentiate one disorder or group of disorders from another taken from the same matrix of qualities. Some disorders are grouped as mood disorders (depression, mania), others are called adjustment reactions; some are ideational aberrations (paranoia, obsessional neurosis), others are limited functional failures of memory (dissociative reaction); some derive from a historical and quite holistic view of personality or character (borderline condition, narcissistic personality) hardly conducive to precise symptom descriptions, others take their cue from a circumscribed habit (alcoholism, fetishism) or a "special symptom" as the DSM-II calls it, such as enuresis or a speech defect. It is clear that not all of these units are just symptoms. It is also clear that if one would like to strive to focus on the symptoms in each category, the word *symptom* teeters between quite different levels of abstraction and precision. And even if one would like to devise a classification system consisting entirely of symptom descriptions, one will still have to reckon with the fact that phenotypical similarity may mask genotypical diversity and, its obverse, that genotypical sameness may be expressed in phenotypical differences.

The language of classification is further compromised and muddled by the fact that it functions as a meeting ground between two very different enterprises. On the one hand it is to serve the nosologists whose task is to conceptualize mental disorders with the greatest possible refinement including the symptoms, course, and etiology of each; on the other hand it is to serve the statisticians whose task is to spot clusters of correlations that confirm or contradict the various "packages" that any given classification contains. Nosologists are, or should be, interested in a precise and clear nomenclature by which mental disorders can be properly named without ambiguity. Statisticians are more likely to be attuned to the overlap of variables between one condition and another, however these are named, on the basis of a great many countings of a great many items —the latter of bewildering diversity. And the clinician is interested in lucid pictures he can match with the salient features of not a disorder or a person but a disordered person!

The Language of Persons

We are now ready to recognize the psychiatrist's third language, the person language he adopts in his clinical work. To put it sharply, and in terms of our previous emphasis on classification, the DSM-II, as all its forebears, is to be used expressly for classifying mental disorders—not patients! The classification scheme is a nosological tool, not an idiom in which to describe patients—apparently a hard lesson to learn. No less a psychiatric luminary than Bleuler objected to the term *dementia praecox* on linguistic grounds, deploring that it could not be turned into a label for the individual patient! Since one cannot speak of *a dementia praecox*, Bleuler sought a term with grammatical flexibility and concocted *schizophrenia* which enables one to speak of *a schizophrenic* and permits adjectival use as well. But that is precisely what should not be allowed, not only on humanitarian grounds but because technically no man or woman is identical with his or her disorder. And such naming is particularly inapt when the disorder itself is as yet only a symptom cluster of unexplained etiology, for many psychiatric patients are free from symptoms for greater or lesser stretches of time. Apart from objections to pejorative labeling that dehumanizes the patient or leads to social ostracism, the point here is that the kind of naming which Bleuler sought to make possible by linguistic means is actually a false labeling.

And this issue is not solved by subsequently inventing qualifying phrases such as *in remission*. When a person is designated as *a* hysteric, or *a* schizophrenic, in remission, logic demands that he be dead or has become a nonperson. What may be in remission is his symptoms on the basis of which a disorder was inferred in the first place and by which the patient is seen as afflicted. Only a disorder or a symptom can be in remission, not the person.

Person language, in psychiatry as anywhere else, is ordinary English (at least for American and British practitioners). Given the high proportion of foreign medical graduates in American psychiatry, it is perhaps not so surprising that ordinary English is so rarely used in the psychiatric description of persons. Foreign-born psychiatrists may find it easier to adopt scientific argot than to learn the subtleties of as complex and idiomatic a language as English, particularly when ease is coupled with the prestige attached to the use of technical terminology. For those not foreign born, ordinary English may seem too unscientific, too common, too easily accessible to laymen, which could—God forbid—include the patients themselves.

And yet, any psychiatrist worth his salt interviews his patients in ordinary English and hears the same language in return—barring occasional jibberish or word salad spoken by severely disturbed patients. His raw data are in this common, unpretentious language. He could and should describe his patients in the same tongue, if only to be able to share his reports with the patients themselves (were he curious and caring enough to seek the patients' verification of his reports) so as to engage with them in an open therapeutic contracting. But, alas, the moment we dictate our reports we seem to spurn good descriptive English in favor of conceptual phrases of a quasi-nosological order, or adapted from the classification system. Many patients are described not as sad, tearful, somber, or downhearted, but right away as *depressed*. Other patients are immediately dubbed *paranoid* when we are only justified in describing their attitude as suspicious or guarded. Instead of calling attention to flamboyant verbiage, histrionic manners, or abruptly changing moods, we take recourse to the term *hysterical*. In lieu of noting and recording the presence of certain rituals, we say *obsessive-compulsive*; a fearful attitude is rendered as *phobic*; a mannerism is labeled *catatonic*. All these words are nosological terms, i.e., adjectives describing a quality of some conceptualized disorder, or classification words. They are adjectival adaptations of listed nouns; they are neither descriptions of the persons before us nor faithful renditions of observed symptoms; they are premature attempts at classification that pigeonhole the person before he or she is faithfully portrayed. These words are clichés loading our reports with the categorizing contents of our own minds. The diagnosis is still to be made, but in recording the history and the psychological examination we have already used categorical words that make verification difficult and thwart communication.

We will have more to say about the language of persons at a later point, but be it noted here that considerable purification of the psychiatrist's mind is needed before he can master this difficult tongue.

The Language of Therapeutic Technique

The fourth psychiatric language in daily use is the language of therapy and therapeutic techniques. Patients tend to be sized up and described according to the interviewer's therapeutic orientation. Psychoanalytic case reports abound with words like *transference, associating, resistance, verbalizing, affect organization,* and *acting out.* Psychopharmacological persuasions come through in *bi-polar depression, dyskinetic,* and details of family trees. Milieu-oriented hospital psychiatric reports dwell on how the patient does in *structured* versus *unstructured* situations and how he reacts to father or mother figures; they specify his *object relations* and pay much attention to *reality contact* and *fantasy formation.* Neuropsychiatric reports speak of *syndromes,* particularly of the temporal lobe and limbic structures, and dwell on *confusion, amnesia,* or *epileptic phenomena,* minutely describing their status or fluctuations and how these are influenced by stressful events, all with an eye on therapeutic alteration of *thresholds.* Custodial hospital reports abound with old-fashioned nosological terms, highly categorical and mostly serving triage functions. Advocates of group therapies lard their assessments with *splitting, identification, loyalty,* and *role.* Transactional analysts adopt the verbiage of family roles; Gestalt therapists focus on *self, speaking out,* and *masking.* And so on. There is an enormous impact of therapy-derived words on the assessment process and what passes for diagnostic descriptions of patients.

The point is not whether this practice is good or bad—we ourselves would argue that scientific data are always a function of the perspective in which they are spotted and formulated. What we wish to indicate here is that the therapeutic perspective entails a special language game which should not be confused with other forms of psychiatric language. All too often the language of therapeutic orientation intrudes upon the language of evaluative description, and eventually upon the language of diagnosis, making them selective or partial at best, and badly skewed, if not muddled, at worst.

The Language of Diagnosis: Official Hodgepodge

Thus far, we have tried to show in a few broad strokes that psychiatry has recourse not to one but to several professional languages and that, in this sense, the name of the psychiatrist could well be Legion. We have also illustrated a prevailing occupational hazard in psychiatry, namely that of unwittingly speaking several languages at the same time, which amounts to a professional paraphasia. Thought and language always interact. Poor thinking leads to poor language use, and faulty habits of speech muddy the clarity of thought. Mere words can feign the existence of entities, and patent phenomena are overlooked when language habits disallow their recognition.

Even when our cautionary remarks in the preceding sections are heeded to the point that we would at least know clearly which language we were speaking at any given moment, we are still running against a formidable barricade in our linguistic housecleaning efforts. Ahead of us looms the spectre of psychiatric diagnosis, a veritable monster of linguistic abuse and obfuscation.

Perhaps the worst feature of diagnostic language is the great artificiality of its form and scope: It consists of a kind of telegraphic speech, highly abbreviated and condensed; typically, it has no verbs, as if to imply that it recognizes no action or process; it consists largely of nouns, noun phrases, and adjectives. While it purports to designate a condition, e.g., alcoholism or hysteria, all too often word choice freezes this condition into a fixed state, stripped of its dynamics, tensions, and process character. Thus, it conjures up entities which the imagination of the user elaborates in some fashion. For diagnostic language does not abbreviate by merely shortening a phrase or by contracting words (e.g., KS for Kansas), but by substituting abstractions and their invented names for a multitude of descriptions (which, as we have seen, are typically far from pure descriptions) and observations (which are often theoretically inspired) via an inference process that may vary from logical step-by-step induction and deduction to an aesthetic, visionary recognition of some mental picture that "matches" an unreflected assortment of phenomena.

A second feature of diagnostic language is that its word-treasure consists of a prescribed nomenclature, which is not just a finite universe of terms but a very small table of permissable words guided by narrow rules for combination and not allowed to grow. While other languages expand, differentiate, and become more versatile, diagnostic language is kept fixed, static, and uniform—whether for good or bad reasons. Due to its narrow bandwidth, it is a language that puts the user before a forced choice situation. The phenomena have to be made to fit the nomenclature, in contrast to ordinary speech and other forms of scientific language which are constantly being adapted to the phenomena and concepts that emerge. The user of a diagnostic manual is not given an opportunity to create the most astute formulation of his patient's conditions or problems, but he is asked to allocate (from *locare*—to place) and assign (i.e., to mark) in order to find the "proper place" for the patient's condition within a list or table. Note that the allocation pertains to the condition, not to the patient! Indeed, to bridge the gap between the condition and the patient, medical parlance takes recourse to the word *case* (from the Latin *casus*—instance). The allocation means, "This case (particular happening) is an instance of such and such (known) condition or illness." The patient himself is not "a case," but his afflication is reasoned to be an instance of a small number of more or less circumscribed conditions earmarked by official names. Again, we are exposing these features of diagnostic language not necessarily to decry them, but to record their peculiarity so as to warn the user of diagnostic terms of their pitfalls. Diagnostic nomenclature is a very odd language form serving a very circumscribed purpose. It is an artificial language game operating in a narrow circle.

A third point of note is that diagnostic language is a compound of diverse conceptions and levels of abstraction. A set of colored blocks of the same shape and size can be sorted according to color differences; each color becomes a rubric. A set of colored blocks of different shapes and sizes can be sorted according to three classes of rubrics: color, shape, size. Of these *color* and *size* contain continuous rubrics allowing measurement, and *shape* contains discontinuous rubrics with only a limited number of forms that allow no transitions. No one would hold that such simple sorting by means of clear variables is possible with mental disorders or medical disease. But the diagnostic categories of psychiatry are very remote indeed from any respectable model; they are an extreme conflation of such diverse groups of variables that one wonders whether they form any coherent order and can be dignified by the word *system*.

Some entries exist by virtue of etiological considerations. Others are explicitly based on the course of the disorder and register an outlook. Still others are squarely based on symptoms or symptom clusters. Etiological groups, moreover, are not of the same order but stem from very diverse etiological theories or visions; symptom groups range from the clear and obvious act of "episodic excessive drinking (of alcohol)" to the fuzziness of "asthenic personality disorder." Behind these very diverse categories lie wholly different language games: Some have to do with brain states; others with psychodynamics; still others with character, adaptation, or social fitness. In some classes, there are allusions to distinctions betweeen acute and chronic states; in others, something is implied about the reversibility or irreversibility of the disorder.

A fourth peculiarity of official diagnostic language is the ambiguity of the recognized genera. For instance, there is a genus *neuroses* and a genus *psychoses*—the latter conditioned by the phrase "not attributed to physical conditions listed previously." How are these genera conceived? Are neuroses and psychoses meant to be seen as continuous in some fashion, e.g., as roughly similar to respectively "mild" and "severe" disorders? If so, what does one do with the currently fashionable syndrome *Borderline State, Condition,* or *Schizophrenia* (for which DSM-II has no entry) when that condition (if it is a circumscribed one) is widely seen as attributable to "personality disorder"? And, indeed, where does the latter fit, if any continuity between classes is assumed? Is there or is there not some hierarchical conception that matches the biological distinctions between class, genus, and species, and puts these factors at discrete levels of abstraction? Or is the diagnostic table only a list, more or less fortuitously assembled in the face of the pragmatic complaints that come the psychiatrist's way, with today different from yesterday, and tomorrow different again? Do geographic locale and cultural milieu play some role in making the list what it is today? Is the list equally useful to private practitioners, military psychiatrists, penological institutions, and the Veterans Administration? Does it address the needs of psychoanalysts as well as state hospitals? If not, there must be something wrong with its over-arching principles and its hierarchical ordering—implict or explicit. Small wonder, then, that each newly proposed diagnostic classification or nomenclature has its friends and foes, and that even its friends feel its use as a kind of professional onus that one has to put up with for the sake of conformity. And no wonder, also, that the language of official diagnosis becomes quickly misused as a kind of fraternity argot, or is perverted into an all-purpose idiom behind which one can hide ignorance or malcontent, particularly when its use adds a little prestige or feigned power.

An extremely important fifth feature of diagnostic language, which it shares with the technical languages of some other disciplines but has graver consequences, is the vulgarization of terms—that nasty process by which technical terms slowly move into the popular domain and lose the qualifications originally put upon their use becoming, in every sense of the word, cheapened. Journalists blithely write of Southeast Asian politics as "schizophrenic." Admirers of R. D. Laing use the same word almost as a term of praise and approval for gifted eccentrics venerated as luminaries. In literature, orderly persons are designated as "compulsives." Hapless compounds of some of our words are made at cocktail parties, such as *egomania*. The Hitlers, Stalins, and Quislings of this world, and indeed Freud himself, are constantly being diagnosed by literati who have never conducted a single psychiatric interview and are unfamiliar with the options in our diagnostic list but love some of our prestigious words. Yesterday it was (take your choice!) bad, or nice, to spot some neurotic traits in public personalities or in members of our social circle; today the epithets must be in the range of the psychoses to have some titillating effect; tomorrow the class of personality disorders will probably be in fashion. Homosexuality has been lifted from the diagnostic manual entirely and is now merely a designation of taste or style. In view of this vulgarization or popularization, one is tempted to quip, "Good riddance!" More temperately, one might say that psychiatry has lost its diagnostic language, which, deplorable as it is, may also be a marvelous opportunity for inventing a new one that will better serve its purpose. We recommend plain English as a viable alternative for the jargon that the public has run away with. Neo-Greek or Neo-Latin is no longer appropriate for designating the disorders which our patients present, if only because they are rarely so packaged that they stand out clearly from all the other features in these persons' lives or circumstances.

With all the frailties, oddities, and artificialities besetting diagnostic language, the psychiatrist is advised to pay heed to its rarefied status and withstand the temptation to use these terms outside the narrow circle of their applicability, if at all!

Other Language Pitfalls in Psychiatry

Though psychiatrists, professionally vowed to be sticklers for words, should be pedagogues of language behavior, they are of course not immune to the twisting or perverting of language that is the common bane of mankind. Speech is an overdetermined function beset by special influences from the id, the superego, the ego-ideal, and the audience, and often poorly managed by the ego.

Upon reading psychiatric reports, one is struck by a number of tendencies which for many writers have become habits. One is to turn an act or a process into a state by word manipulation, e.g., the apt word *relation* is changed into the inapt word *relationship*. Another bad habit is overprecision that becomes ponderous redundancy, e,g., *ego defense* for *defense*. Poor theoretical grounding leads to the misuse of *acting out* for *enacting* or *making manifest in behavior*. Moralization comes through in such words as *perversion, psychopathic, inadequate personality, infantile personality,* and *character disorder.* Outright accusatory expressions are *castrating female, passive father, penis envy,* and *schizophrenogenic mother.* All too many psychiatric words have inapt space connotation: *borderline personality, underlying, ego boundaries, splitting, facade.* Words for the functions of conscience always stress its proscriptive side in general terms, i.e., *strict* or *demanding,* and rarely address its prescriptive aspect, as if to imply that conscience is only a damper rather than an organizer of behavior. Some word usage is tendentious: *compulsive* for *orderly, depressed* for *sad.*

Grossly inadequate use is made in many psychiatric reports of the words *appearing* and *seeming.* Misuse of these terms allows the writer to have definite opinions but to soften these in his presentation as well as to have no opinion but to give the impression of having one. Reports abound in "the patient seems to . . . ," "it seems that . . . ," "the patient appears to be . . . ," and "it appears that . . ." —all used interchangeably. *Appearing* is definite; it refers to something becoming clear and visible. But, in the mind of some users, it becomes associated with appearance, in the sense of mere semblance. *To seem* is less definite than *to appear.* The word *seem* implies that a particular beholder has as yet only an impression and is aware of his own subjectivity. Profuse use of these weasel words in psychiatric reports indicates that the writer equivocates between objectivity and subjectivity, between fantasy and reality, or between impressions and facts, pleading with the reader that he be allowed to have his cake and eat it. The psychiatrist who overloads his reports with such weasel words shows that he is under some strain to force his observations into the mold of some diagnostic category, building up a plausible case for the eventual diagnostic allocation he will make. Or else he has already put the patient intuitively into some pigeonhole (which may prove to be correct) and is now proceeding to see the patient from that nosological angle so as to achieve a good fit. These are some of the vagaries of allocating, fitting, and matching that the use of diagnostic nomenclature imposes, much to the discredit of the profession.

Diagnosis and the Difference It Makes

Much of the preceding exposition and criticism of psychiatric language(s) could induce one to adopt an antidiagnostic attitude or to advocate an adiagnostic position. This notion is far from our intention. We believe that diagnosis is not only a necessary psychiatric activity, but by far the most important single *raison d'être* for psychiatry as a profession. Members of many different professions as well as laymen have much to offer in alleviating the plight of the mentally ill, the emotionally disturbed, the psychologically disorganized, and—in the broadest sense—those who have difficulty in coping with the stresses and strains of life. Many interventions are possible and indeed are offered by a veritable army of eager workers. But unfortunately many interventions are made available and tried out without the least concern for their fitness to the condition to which they are being applied.

Many treatments are available on a self-referral basis, without prior diagnostic assessment and without explicit prescription. How much better use could be made of these treatments if some expert were available to match a defined condition with a judiciously chosen remedy by way of a logical and specific prescription! It is our belief that whatever psychiatrists may now wish to do or come to do in the future, their single most useful and desirable function lies in making diagnostic assessments that can be understood by diverse therapists and formulating prescriptions that map out specific therapeutic strategies and modalities.

Inherent in this proposition is the whole issue of specificity both of mental disorder and of therapy. The theory and practice of drug therapy highlights extremes on both sides of this issue. Not long ago when tranquilizers arrived, they were thought to apply very broadly to a great variety of mental disorders as a palliative for their commonest symptom: anxiety. They were widely prescribed for conditions that were not probed and differentiated, indeed hardly diagnosed at all, in the belief that anxiety, as the vaguest common denominator, could be lessened. To many prescribers diagnosis was not really needed since neither specificity of disorder nor specificity of remedy was deemed relevant. Today, however, for the use of a drug such as Lithium the greatest acumen is required in diagnosing the specific syndrome of bipolar depression, and even the prevailing phase thereof, in order to formulate a precise dosage. Thus, in psychopharmacology, we have moved in a few decades from general to specific treatment, with an increasing demand for precise diagnostic work and minutely calibrated prescription.

Many psychiatric conditions lie somewhere between the two extremes of generality and specificity. So do the therapies. If the psychiatrist's diagnostic ability is to be singled out as his professional forte and his most useful asset from a social point of view, everything will hinge on his articulateness in formulating a clear, pointed, and useful diagnostic summary of the condition presented by the patient, so that it can and will lead to a well-considered prescription which is not merely pragmatic or opportunistic but follows logically from his understanding of the patient's malady or problem.

What kind of language is required for such an endeavor? It seems to us, first, that diagnosing by merely naming the disorder will not do, if only because the currently officially listed disorders cover too wide a range from the specific to the general and from definite to vague formulations. Moreover, the patient's presenting complaints and symptoms are often so complex or unique that trying to fit them to the extant list may lead to their falsification. But perhaps more importantly, in the present state of psychiatric science, the naming of disorders in terms of the standard nomenclature gives insufficient clues to treatment. A language must be found that summarily describes the patient's disorder in such a way that many would-be helpers and adjudicators are informed by the condition and can be helped to calculate its impact.

Secondly, if diagnosing is to make a difference, as this conference holds, it will have to evolve into the science and art of prescribing. Here we have to face the fact that the semblance of unity and systematization present in psychiatric nosology, though still only a semblance, contrasts favorably with the rampant eclecticism and fierce disunity of psychiatric therapeutics. To put it more crassly, much psychiatric treatment, even after thoughtful diagnosis, is ad hoc, opportunistic, pragmatic, or overly and sometimes solely determined by what the would-be therapist knows or likes to do. At its best, there are volumes on various therapies and organized schools in which various therapists are educated, but we lack a unitary, comprehensive theory of psychiatric treatment. Even the most prestigious general psychiatric handbooks contain only separate chapters on selective modes of treatment, presented staccato, each being a forum for a special point of view and unrelated to one another. It is not surprising, therefore, that engagement in one therapy or another is often not instigated by a prescription, for knowledgeable prescribing should be undergirded by a comprehensive theory of therapeutics. The science and art of prescribing are perched between and atop two large intellectual enterprises: diagnosis (including nosology, taxonomy, and nomenclature) and therapeutics (including all remedies, particular approaches, and a theory of intervention and change).

Given his army of diagnostic and therapeutic specialists, the psychiatrist is somewhat in the position of a broker between various parties—patients, relatives, referral persons and agencies, institutions of various kinds, and many other caretakers and therapists.

If his technical jargon pleases one of these parties, it is sure to displease others; if some understand his formulations, surely others do not; if his diagnoses instigate hope in some, they lead to despair or callousness in others. Brokerage requires skill, particularly in communication.

Shall the psychiatrist therefore become a wizard in languages, skillfully switching from one language to the other as he addresses his various parties to give each one his due? Unfortunately, his professional life does not allow him to be available to all relevant parties at once, like an interpreter at the United Nations. Yes, his situation does call for linguistic versatility and the skill of a polyglot, at times, to use the language that is appropriate to the situation. But his situations are so diverse, his actual and potential audiences so many, that it would be much better if he adopted from the start and maintained throughout his work the one language most likely to be understood by the largest diversity of people and the least likely to be misunderstood by anyone—the mother tongue. For psychiatric purposes, the mother tongue is the most viable professional instrument of communication. It is to be used deftly, tersely, clearly, and with precision. As the old Hebrew preacher put it: "Let thy speech be short, comprehending much in a few words" (Ecclesiasticus 32:8 [Apocrypha]). Or as Hemingway (1947) put it three thousand years later: "The first and most important thing of all . . . is to strip language clean, to lay it bare down to the bone" (p. 983).

After all, Legion was healed only after he stopped twisting words, and after the swine had taken his obscure utterances away with them to their graves.

References

AMERICAN PSYCHIATRIC ASSOCIATION: *Diagnostic and Statistical Manual of Mental Disorders*, Second Edition. Washington, D.C.: Author, 1968.

BLEULER, EUGEN (1911): *Dementia Praecox or the Group of Schizophrenias*, Joseph Zinken, tr. New York: International Universities Press, 1950.

HEMINGWAY, ERNEST: Quoted from *Paris Was Our Mistress* by Samuel Putnam (New York: Viking Press, 1947) in *Familiar Quotations*, Ed. 13, by John Bartlett. Boston: Little, Brown, 1955.

MENNINGER, KARL *et al.*: *The Vital Balance*. New York: Viking Press, 1963.

PROVOCATIVE ISSUES IN PSYCHIATRIC DIAGNOSIS:

A Dialogue*

FREDERICK SHECTMAN, Ph.D.†

In what follows I seek to deal with the major issues in psychiatric diagnosis by means of a dialogue format. My aim is that the reader be more involved by having an antagonist of diagnosis raise doubts and express criticisms, while a proponent of diagnosis responds to these challenges.

I am intrigued by your title and wonder what you mean by provocative since that word has more than one meaning.

Precisely, and I use it in two ways. On the one hand, the whole idea of psychiatric diagnosis is one that angers or provokes many people, as you well know. On the other hand, the topic is provocative in that it arouses and stimulates thinking and feeling in a productive fashion. And it is in this second sense that I wish us to talk—generating, I hope, more light than heat.

* This paper relies heavily on ideas discussed elsewhere (Shevrin & Shectman 1973; Shectman 1973). The author would also like to express his appreciation to Drs. Ann Appelbaum, Michael Harty, Howard Shevrin, and Sydney Smith for their helpful comments and suggestions.

† Core Psychologist, Diagnostic Service, The Menninger Foundation; Member, Training Committee, Postdoctoral Training Program in Clinical Psychology; Faculty Member, Menninger School of Psychiatry; Psychotherapy Supervisor, Menninger School of Psychiatry, The Menninger Foundation, Topeka, Kansas.

Nicely said; that is my wish, too. But much is at stake here for these are heartfelt issues.

Agreed, for without passion there is no truth.

I am pleased that you mention passion because, along with Carl Rogers (1951), my concern is that diagnosis is overly intellectual as well as too concerned with the past. I am heartened by the new encounter movements where time is not wasted in abstract diagnostic formulations and history taking, and where use of one's intellect is avoided in favor of the immediacy of direct experience undiluted by thought (Back 1972). Advocates of this approach object to the overemphasis on reason which can stifle feeling and thereby bypass the core of a person's experience.

Although that orientation seeks to compensate for the onesidedness you mention, surely you are not in favor of abandoning reason altogether? An ". . . overemphasis on reason is not an inherent part of diagnosis but a poor diagnostic practice. . . . By seeming to force a choice between experiencing and understanding, encounter groups act as if to be rational prevents one from being a 'feeling' person" (Shevrin & Shectman 1973, p. 453). This dialectic is indicative of the current, widespread anti-intellectual movement which confuses using one's intellect with intellectualization. It is one thing to use one's intellect to understand, quite another to use it to prevent oneself from having feelings. But to discard both uses in order to get rid of the latter one is hardly warranted. If you repudiate diagnosis because understanding can be misused, you deny what you stand for, i.e., the person's experience, because part of his experience is his thinking, reasoning, and understanding.

But that effort at understanding in itself spoils the experience!

That is a curious viewpoint you offer. "For, if understanding broadens and deepens what we are, then it can only spoil what we do not want to have understood, e.g., something irrational. . . . [Your attitude] is somewhat like the heavy smoker who reads that smoking may cause cancer—and who then decides to give up reading because that knowledge interferes with his enjoyment of smoking" (Shevrin & Shectman 1973, p. 453).

Closer to home, "There is . . . a more recent, more militant, more desperate, and more dangerous extension of the 'I know how you feel' to the 'I know how you feel and therefore I know how to treat you'. . . . A diabetic patient certainly knows better how it feels to adjust his life to dietary restrictions and insulin injections than does his attending physician, but should he therefore regulate his neighbor's insulin regimen? Yet, strangely enough, this is in essence what happens in some leaderless, nongoal-directed encounter groups in which unselected participants 'confront' each other in an effort to reduce the anxiety of their loneliness and to 'get closer' to other people" (Bauer 1971, p. 472).

But you must agree that some people are too intellectualizing and emotionally inhibited and need to be more in touch with their feelings if they are to grow psychologically.

I do indeed concur. But ". . . there is good reason to think that the prevailing psychopathology of our time and our culture is no longer typified by constriction and hyper-repression, but rather by weakness of impulse control, narcissistic self-indulgence, loose thought organization, and externalization of conflicts. . . . Here, then, is a jarring note: many of the newer and somewhat faddist therapies address themselves in theory and presuppositions to more or less Victorian psychopathologies, while many of the clients they attract, by a kind of drift in the absence of diagnostic screening, may possess the opposite kind of pathology requiring remedies toward containment and restructuring rather than fitful abreactions" (Pruyser 1973, pp. 435–36). If different kinds of therapies attract different clienteles because of self-selection, the lack of proper diagnosis leaves the way open for a mismatch between the patient and the type of treatment best suited to his needs. Moreover, not only may patients be self-selected but therapists may be as well—with the potential dangers Bauer (1971) implies. Without a way of taking individual differences into account and tailoring treatment requirements accordingly, you are vulnerable to violating those humanistic interests in people as separate persons which you, as an encounter-emotive enthusiast, so value.

But if the diagnostician is in the powerful position of matching patients and treatment, he is also in a position to exercise much socially sanctioned influence. I am worried about the social-political implications of control, by society in general and by special interest groups in particular, of which the diagnostician may be a willing or unwitting agent. I am thinking of the recent Donaldson judgment (McDonald 1975) about involuntary hospitalization and the Wyatt v. Anderhold case (Stickney 1974) involving the "right to treatment." As you know, in the Donaldson case the United States Supreme Court ruled that a psychiatric patient cannot be involuntarily hospitalized with only custodial care if he is not dangerous and can function outside a hospital. And in the Wyatt case, a United States Court of Appeals reaffirmed the principle of "right to treatment" as a matter of constitutional law ("Decision Reached on Wyatt: U. S. Court of Appeals Reaffirms Right to Treatment" 1975)—a ruling that has already led to defining and setting minimum standards of treatment.

Like you, I am in favor of decisions that safeguard patients' rights against misapplied political power. But such legal decisions can only make diagnosis more important, not less. For example, as a result of the *Donaldson* case it will now be even more necessary to determine who does and who does not need to be hospitalized because he is likely to be "dangerous." In fact, defining the term *dangerous* involves diagnosis. Concerned people are already asking whether the "dangerous" category includes only those who pose a physical threat or does it also include those unable to care for themselves and are a danger because of forgetfulness, inattentiveness, or poor judgment, like the infirm and the senile. The understandable tendency is to play it safe and keep the patient in the hospital to avoid being blamed, if not sued, in case the patient does cause some harm once he is released. But, as these legal cases show, such tendencies can lead to abuse. Now, however, the error could be in the other direction—discharging the patient too hastily to avoid being sued for unjustly or unnecessarily hospitalizing him. The only way to avoid this Scylla and Charybdis is to have solid diagnostic work on which to base these knotty decisions. It is a similar story in regard to the *Wyatt* decision, for it necessitates, as a right to treatment, an individualized treatment plan, among other things. Without individualized diagnostic understanding that is applicable to treatment planning, how can such a plan be devised?

These cases remind me of Thomas Szasz's (1961, 1970, 1974) posi-tion that what masquerades as diagnosis can really be a social-judg-mental way of stigmatizing certain people and that hospitals can be used as jails to incarcerate those people who act in certain unpopular ways. His viewpoint reminds me of how the Chinese use "thought reform" camps and how the Russians employ "treatment centers" for their dissenters. And you need only read Solzhenitsyn's (1974) The Gulag Archipelago *to know what I mean.*

I do know what you mean. However, I would not say ". . . that Szasz is right or wrong, for he might be either, depending upon the circumstances in a particular case, but by tarring all diagnoses with the same brush, he acts as if this misuse were built into diag-nosis, rather than being an abuse of it. To do away with diagnosis because it can be misapplied is tantamount to abolishing surgery because some physicians perform unethical or unnecessary opera-tions" (Shevrin & Shectman 1973, p. 459).

By resorting to overkill and attacking the harmfulness of all psychiatric diagnosis, Szasz obscures as much as he clarifies. In fact, he may wreak as much chaos and do as much if not more harm as those whom he attacks by frightening away the very persons who most need psychiatric help, e.g., people in turmoil and on the verge of irreversible action, like murder or suicide. In short, Szasz's resorting to philosophical and linguistic cleverness to claim that mental illness is a myth only reinforces the existing fears and re-sistances of people who are already ambivalent about seeking help for their distress. And ". . . to be logical is not to be right . . . and nothing on God's earth could ever make it right" (Mann 1961, p. 134). But, actually, I do not think Szasz is as logical as he is ingeniously deceptive; and there is a difference between ingenuity and truth and that distinction must be preserved! Expressing confidence that the truth will out, Freud (1927) said, "The voice of the intellect is a soft one, but it does not rest till it has gained a hearing" (p. 53).

Condemning Szasz and involking God and even Freud! Your ire is indeed raised. Pardon me for saying so, but could it be that part of your anger is due to Szasz's arguments having a kernel of painful truth in them?

Perhaps so, for one ". . . point implicit in Szasz' criticism is that where there is no clear body of agreed upon and established scientific knowledge about what constitutes psychiatric disturbance and treatment, the way is open to abuses of the kind he notes" (Shevrin & Shectman 1973, p. 459). I am pained by how far the helping professions still have to go in developing and linking adequate diagnostic criteria to treatment planning. Actually, however, I am more troubled that it has taken an external pressure to get clinicians to address themselves to this issue—especially since they are experts in helping others to see the need for self-motivation and responsibility.

But they are also being tolerant by realizing that such shifts are not easily accomplished. At any rate, by "external pressure" I presume you are referring to third-party insurers and to the Professional Standard Review Organizations or PSRO as they are called.

Yes. As you know, PSRO came into being in October 1972 when the United States Congress passed and the president signed into law Public Law 92-603, specifically section 249-F which requires both utilization review and monitoring of the institutional medical care provided for Medicare and Medicaid patients as well as beneficiaries of Maternal and Child Health programs.

I also know that many doctors fear the consequences of that legislation. Claude Welch (1974), chairman of the American Medical Association's Task Force on Guidelines of Care, notes that ". . . overutilization, particularly of diagnostic services, adds enormously to costs" (p. 1319). The expectable tendency, then, would be to curtail diagnosis in psychiatry—especially in view of the opposition to it that already exists and the questions concerning its utility and even potential harmfulness, as we have been discussing. And, by the way, what would be so terrible about that anyway?

Well, for one thing the demand to cut costs is opposed by the doctor's need to protect himself if he is to be held legally accountable —a pressure that could lead to an excess of diagnostic services, mainly for the clinician's protection, just as doctors who treat physical ailments have done in response to the increasing number of medical malpractice suits. In the pull of opposing forces I fear that the patient and his needs may be lost and that arbitrariness may override judgment. Another "cost" may be that the quality of care may be reduced by the demands of PSRO. "The publication of criteria will tend to standardize all procedures, will lock medicine into a mold and ultimately prevent flexibility and progress; that is the essence of cookbook medicine" (Welch 1974, p. 1319). Moreover, Robert Gibson (1974), a pioneer in coordinating the relationship between PSRO and psychiatry, asserts, "The PSRO system has been formulated more to deal with medical and surgical cases than with psychiatric ones. The approach is primarily directed toward reducing utilization, not improving quality. There is a distinct danger that it may introduce a cost-effectiveness attitude that destroys the essential human quality so necessary to psychiatric treatment. It is small wonder that psychiatrists view the whole business with distrust" (p. 41). In other words, the increasing emphasis on and demand for accountability could paradoxically undermine PSRO's prime goal—namely, good diagnosis and treatment. My point is that the existence of PSRO is, in part, an example of the general, growing move toward consumerism today—e.g., accessibility of educational and medical records, growth of patients' rights movements, and increasing numbers of malpractice suits.

But what's so wrong with all that?

Greater openness and accessibility of information may feel good, but, as I implied earlier, what feels good does not necessarily make good sense. With all this openness and information sharing, what will become of privacy, selective sharing, and confidentiality? These ingredients are essential in a psychiatric relationship if the clinician is truly to understand and formulate plans to help another human being—which is my definition of diagnosis. More properly, I mean "... diagnosing, to indicate its transitive, continuing nature, its look toward the future rather than toward something static or past" (Menninger 1974–1975, p. 9). As an unfolding process, diagnosing needs safeguards against those social controls that handicap it. You see, my concern is not only that diagnosis can be misused for social-political reasons but also that well-intentioned but misguided social-political motives can lead to an abuse of diagnosis!

I see what you mean—it can cut both ways. But I hope you agree that, as a standard setting enterprise, PSRO may not only help curtail

the kind of abuses to which Szasz refers but also help advance psy-
chiatry by developing criteria and norms as a first step in establishing
accepted standards for what constitutes psychiatric disturbance, ade-
quate diagnosis, and proper treatment.

I do indeed agree.

Good! I, too, think PSRO can advance psychiatry by doing away
with faulty classification which parades as sophisticated scientific
diagnosis. What I mean is that patients who are assigned to any
particular nosological category (e.g., schizophrenia) vary considerably
within that group, and this variability clearly demonstrates that the
classification does not refer to one specific entity. Thus, diagnosis
obscures as much as it informs—maybe more—because it provides
a false sense of security about having accurately conveyed some-
thing important about how the individual patient placed in that
nosological category is understood. Hence, diagnosis is defective
and useless, if not actually misleading.

I realize that in challenging you thus I am moving away from my
previous criticism of diagnosis as being overly rational. Now I am
indeed concerned that psychiatric diagnosis is not very scientific,
i.e., not rational enough. I am also suggesting to you that pigeonholing
a person obscures his individuality, and the violation of individuality
is a concern you yourself expressed earlier.

I do not mind if you change your positions at all, for I am pleased
that you take our talk seriously enough to confront me from various
viewpoints. As for your challenges, however, you are objecting not
to diagnosis but to labeling. "This line of thought misses the very
essence of diagnosis which is to determine ways in which each
patient differs from the model or ideal type. These departures from
the norm reflect the patient's individuality. . . . As Alexander has
noted, 'What the therapist is primarily interested in is not the nosological classification of a person, not in what way he is similar to others
but in what way he differs from them'. . . . The point is that it is a
misapplication of diagnosis to expect the patients' disturbances to
fall neatly into classical nosological categories. This error is compounded by then objecting to diagnosis because such reifications of
ideal types do not apply to each case and are thus invalid. This

apparent lack of validity occurs because of a narrow and misleading conception of diagnosis. The fact is that individual disturbances do not correspond to ideal types in textbooks because only ideal types based on general principles appear in textbooks. Otherwise, the latter would be little more than endless catalogues or listings of individual variations of little use to the student who wants to understand a particular patient in terms of general principles and how his deviations particularize him. The 'label' as such should serve as a beginning, not an end point in diagnosis—because once the broad nosological category is determined it then becomes crucial to delineate in what ways the particular patient fits and does not fit the abstract ideal type" (Shevrin & Shectman 1973, p. 462).

It is in this sense that the axiom " 'The better a clinician knows a patient, the harder it is to make a diagnosis' " (Strauss 1973, p. 447) applies. As Menninger and his colleagues (1963) assert: ". . . even more important than the treatment is skillful diagnosis. But this means diagnosis in a new sense, not the mere application of a label. It is not a search for a proper name by which one can refer to this affliction in this and other patients. It is diagnosis in the sense of understanding just how the patient is ill and how ill the patient is, how he became ill and how his illness serves him. From this knowledge one may draw logical conclusions regarding how changes might be brought about in or around the patient which would affect his illness" (pp. 6–7).

How does PSRO relate to all this?

Well, first of all, ". . . PSRO will be required to develop norms of care based upon typical patterns of practice in its regions (including typical lengths of stay for institutional care by age and diagnosis) as principal points of evaluation and review. [Secondly] Data profiles are required for patients and providers of services and are to be reviewed regularly to determine whether the care and services ordered or rendered are consistent with acceptable PSRO criteria" (Sullivan 1974, pp. 1354–55). My hope is that such practices will lead to real diagnosis—that is, enable psychiatry to ascertain better what problems in what patient, with what family, and what environment can be understood (diagnosed) by what clinician with what method in what setting, leading to what predictions about what outcome.

That is a tall order!

True, but there are already beginnings. For example, the results of the Menninger Foundation's Psychotherapy Research Project are a step toward diagnostic specification along individual lines based on assessment of various psychological functions (Horwitz 1974).

Lest you become overly optimistic, I would remind you that "Psychiatry is in a particularly precarious position because of the inherent difficulties in valuating, quantifying, and documenting the efficacy of psychiatric care. Traditional techniques utilizing the review of individual cases, conferences, and study of charts are inadequate for meeting the kind of demands now being made. For example, the PSRO legislation requires that standards of care be developed through profiles for usual length of stay and appropriateness of treatment. Such information is simply not available for the treatment of psychiatric illness; it may not even be possible to develop such meaningful criteria. Such issues as the motivation of the patient, variation in treatment approaches, and differing goals of treatment lead to wide differences" (Gibson 1974, p. 41). For example, I wonder how much time a PSRO would permit for the treatment of a patient whose problem is that he unconsciously wants to defeat those who seek to help him?

Your question makes me smile. It is just such individual differences that will have to be diagnosed in order to allow for documentation on which to base more accurate predictions of why it is likely that one patient will need to be treated differently or longer or shorter than another patient with the same typological diagnosis. It is because PSRO will require norms and profiles for patients, clinicians, and institutions that the issue of intragroup variability will be highlighted—a process, as I said, that can lead to true diagnosis of the individual patient. So rather than fear that psychiatric diagnosis will be exposed as useless, I am cautiously optimistic that PSRO will require psychiatrists to sharpen their thinking and skills and to upgrade their diagnostic acumen.

My fear, however, is that many clinicians have not really been committed to the diagnostic enterprise for just the reasons we have been discussing. And without commitment and adequate training and with clinicians engaging in diagnostic work primarily to satisfy a requirement and protect themselves legally, poor diagnostic practice may well result. That stance could further undermine the already weakened position of diagnosis, because the minimal value it would have under such conditions could be mistaken as an inherent limitation of diagnostic work in general.

Based on your concern for individual understanding, I assume you agree with "humanists" like me who ". . . maintain that every person should be considered in his own uniqueness and individuality, and that no one should be stripped of his dignity by being assigned classificatory labels that represent general characteristics more or less shared by groups of people" (Weiner 1972, p. 537). As Maslow (1966), generally credited with being the founder of the humanistic movement, says ". . . I must approach a person as an individual unique and peculiar, the sole member of his class" (p. 10).

Wait a moment! "A clinician does not have to forego attention to an individual's uniqueness simply because he identifies some characteristics that the individual shares in common with other people and which suggest some diagnostic classification. How an individual is like other people and how he is different from them are complementary bits of information that the clinician can and should use together in his efforts to understand and help his patients. It furthermore cannot be overlooked that the price of disavowing classification can be very steep. As soon as similarities between people as expressed in classificatory labels are dispensed with, cumulative clinical wisdom becomes impossible" (Weiner 1972, p. 538). In other words, ". . . if we are all so unique, would it not be impossible to establish general principles of human nature and to learn and to be able to generalize? Would we not be totally ignorant of how to help each new patient if all previous ones were also unique" (Shevrin & Shectman 1973, p. 463)? Gough (1971) puts it concisely: ". . . a therapist should not in glorious ignorance or indifference recapitulate the errors, false starts, mistakes, and miscalculations of past relationships with each new patient. To build rationally on past experience, a method for relating the new to the old is needed, and this bridge is precisely what diagnosis is intended to supply" (p. 163).

Furthermore, are not the humanists guilty of the very judgmental and stigmatizing behavior that they so decry? By calling themselves "humanists," do they not imply that others are not humanistically inclined and thereby subtly label them?

I will let other humanists answer those questions. I want to turn our discussion to two other issues concerning diagnosis—its questionable reliability and validity. Pasamanick et al. (1959) state, "Any number of studies have indicated that psychiatric diagnosis is at present so unreliable as to merit very serious question when classifying, treating and studying patient behavior and outcome" (p. 127). And others (e.g., Kreitman et al. 1961) agree.

But others have also studied this issue and have reached different conclusions. Beck (1962), for example, asserts that nosology is only one of many factors which can reduce reliability and increase variability. A recent study (Kendell 1973) supports this contention by demonstrating that reliability increases markedly when such factors as differences in degree of clinicians' training and experience are taken into account. Furthermore, Pasamanick et al. (1959) note that unreliability can be due to differences in psychiatrists' theoretical orientations, and the results of the United States-United Kingdom joint diagnostic study (Cooper et al. 1972) highlight just that point.

I am sure I can find additional references in the professional literature to rebut yours and that we could go back and forth. However, the fact that there are such contradictory findings should in itself persuade you to abandon diagnosis because it is unreliable.

Good point! "But is such unreliability a basis for doing away with diagnosis? Or is it not instead a reason for redoubling our efforts to refine diagnosis so as to make it more useful" (Shervin & Shectman 1973, p. 463)? Menninger et al. (1963) state that they ". . . vigorously oppose the view that treatment, other than first aid, should proceed before or without diagnosis. On the contrary . . . diagnosis is today more important than ever. The very fact that psychiatric designations have become so meaningless by conflicting usage makes it more rather than less necessary that we approach the specific problem of illness with a cautious, careful scrutiny and appraisal that has characterized the best medical science since the early days. It is still necessary to know in advance, to plan as logically as we can, what kind of interference with a human life we propose to make" (p. 6). And, again, the results of the Menninger Foundation's landmark psychotherapy study apply: ". . . the Psychotherapy Research Project had an influence on the practice of psychotherapy and psychoanalysis at the Menninger Foundation both in large and small ways. One definite finding which . . . infiltrated into our thinking and practice was the importance of a careful diagnostic study before embarking upon treatment, particularly psychoanalysis. Despite the current popularity of the new briefer therapies, there is still considerable conviction at our institution, reinforced by the present study, that analysis is an unrivaled method for the alteration of deep-seated character problems. But the research impressed upon us the great care that must be taken in the selection of cases for such treatment lest we expend much effort, time, and money to no avail" (Horwitz 1974, p. xxi).

But really, what is the necessity of having a diagnostic understanding in advance? The important aspects of the patient and his disturbance will emerge in the course of treatment anyway, and the treater can then modify his treatment approach accordingly.

Things are more complicated than that. What the therapist selects to attend to depends upon his theoretical framework, especially his explanations for what causes psychiatric disturbance. An organically oriented therapist will see something quite different from a dynamically inclined one, even if they interview the same patient. Because their cognitive sets are different, different interventions will flow from their different explanations. "These interventions in themselves alter the functioning under observation and shape the feedback from what is observed and thereby change what is observed from then on" (Shevrin & Shectman 1973, p. 464). As Laing (1969) says: "A doctor does not usually feel he intervenes . . . in the processes of, say, cardiovascular failure, or tuberculosis, simply by hearing the complaint, taking a history, doing an examination. He has not started to intervene with a view to *change* until he begins his treatment, *after* he has done all that is necessary to arrive at his diagnosis. In our case, we are intervening in and changing the situation *as soon as* we are involved. As soon as we interplay with the situation, we have already begun to intervene. . . . At a particular time one is inclined to define the situation in a particular way. . . . Our definition is an act of intervention that changes the situation, which thus requires redefining; it introduces a new factor. At any moment of time, in the continuous process of looking through, of diagnosis, we see it in a particular way that leads us to a nondefinitive definition, subject to revision in the light of the transformations that this very definition induces, prospectively and retrospectively. Medically, our diagnosis does not affect the fact that the person has tuberculosis. We do not change the illness by our diagnosis" (pp. 39–41). This interdependence between one's understanding of the patient's functioning and the effects of interventions based on that understanding cannot be overlooked.

In short, your assertion is that ". . . since everything is bound to come out in treatment anyway, why bother with diagnosis separate from treatment. The point is that once explaining begins, interventions occur which modify what is subsequently observed. 'Everything' does not emerge, for the unsolicited observation of unselected functioning clearly never occurs" (Shevrin & Shectman 1973, p. 464). As Laing (1969) says: "Diagnosis *begins* as soon as one encounters a particular situation, and never ends. The way one sees through the situation changes the situation. As soon as we convey in any way (by a gesture, a handshake, a cough, a smile, an inflection of our voice) what we see or think we see, *some* change is occurring even in the most rigid situation" (p. 40). From this standpoint, "The crux of the matter becomes, then, how explicit the clinician is in his observations and questions, how systematic he is in pursuing hypotheses which clarify and raise new questions, and at what point in his work with the patient he does this. Does he do it only after some not very well thought through interventions do not work leaving him and the patient dissatisfied? Or does he do it before formal treatment is undertaken—in fact, using his prior understanding to shape treatment? It is the latter way of thinking which Cameron . . . had in mind when he regarded diagnosis as '. . . a design for action. This statement—that diagnosis is a design for action— is simply part of the general statement that the question, "What is it?", is always bound up with its twin question, "What am I going to do about it?" ' . . . As such, diagnosis generates a program for doing something 'about it' which flows from answering the question, 'What is it?' " (Shevrin & Shectman 1973, p. 472). From this standpoint, it is impossible not to diagnose, if by diagnosis one means understanding well enough to move in one direction rather than another in helping the patient.

All right, it is impossible not to diagnose. But let's talk specifically about how psychiatrists diagnose. In particular, I am referring to the Rosenhan (1973) experiment, "On Being Sane in Insane Places."

I was afraid you would bring up that study.

And well you should be! For in discussing how eight people pretending to be mentally ill were admitted to and discharged from twelve different mental hospitals without being detected as imposters, Rosenhan mounts a frontal attack on psychiatric diagnosis by questioning its ability to judge the difference between "normal" and "abnormal."

I was afraid, not because the study is embarrassing, but rather because it confuses as well as clarifies and, like Szasz's work, can more aptly be called "On Being Misinformed by Misleading Arguments" (Shectman 1973).

Frankly, I am tiring of your criticalness. Here is a concrete example of the failure and harmfulness of diagnosis. It is your viewpoint that must be defended now, not someone else's!

Fair enough. But in so doing I hope to tie together many of the issues we have discussed. For example, Rosenhan reports that the pseudopatients were diagnosed as either schizophrenic or, in one case, manic-depressive. "*But were they really diagnosed or simply labeled?* This question is no mere splitting of semantic hairs, but is at the heart of the problem. The pseudopatients were obviously categorized on the basis of their reported symptom—auditory hallucinations. . . . [But as I said earlier] A psychiatric label . . . should serve as a beginning, not an end point, in diagnosis. . . . Otherwise, automatically applied labels lead to mechanistically applied [diagnoses and] treatments, e.g., complaints of hearing voices equals schizophrenia [equals hospitalization] equals a prescription for medication. . . . Rosenhan correctly puts his finger on poor diagnostic practice, but he [makes the mistake of concluding] . . . that psychiatric diagnosis [itself is the villain]. . . . An abuse of diagnosis is not an indictment of the enterprise of diagnosis . . . but Rosenhan [like Szasz, equates the two] . . . as if poor practice of diagnosis means it should be given up. This is as illogical as demanding an end to violin music on the grounds that many people play the instrument poorly" (Shectman 1973, p. 523).

But Rosenhan also aptly describes the harmful effect of pejorative labeling.

To repeat myself, misuse of diagnosis is not an indictment of diagnosis itself. Certainly a label, applied or acted upon in a pejorative way, compounds the troubles of already troubled people. Moreover, "Rosenhan may claim that it is the process of labeling which exerts such a deleterious effect upon the individual's life. The practicing psychiatrist, on the other hand, will at once be able to call to mind many patients whom he has seen in second or third attacks of schizophrenic illness whose first attacks were not recognized or diagnosed . . ." (Ostow 1973, p. 361). My point is that severely disturbed people are troubled long before they receive psychiatric labels; the nature of their disturbance is what most seriously limits them, not the label. Furthermore, there is evidence to suggest: (1) that stigmatization due to psychiatric hospitalization is overemphasized (Gove & Fain 1973); (2) that the disturbed or socially deviant person is often stigmatized as such long before he is hospitalized, not afterward, and that this stigmatization itself frequently leads to hospitalization (Levinson et al. 1967); and (3) that people were stigmatized long before diagnostic labels were developed.

Rosenhan also describes how the various mental hospital staffs contented themselves with describing the actions of the pseudopatients without ever encountering them and interacting with them as fellow human beings.

Agreed. In each case, the hospital staff focused on the pseudopatient's behavior rather than his inner experience. They thus missed the opportunity to diagnose the patient's capacity to form a "diagnostic alliance," i.e., the patient's ability to work in a collaborative way with other people in order to understand himself better and to aid in planning treatment. This issue is crucial in distinguishing good diagnostic practice which leads to appropriate treatment from poor practice which yields only a static label. Indeed, "The necessity for taking into account the patient's experience of his disturbance is at the very core of diagnosis, for otherwise the patient becomes [Rogers's and Szasz's passive] ... object who is acted upon rather than a person who is actively engaged and understood. By not recognizing this distinction, the 'diagnosticians' in Rosenhan's study saw their task as identifying the problem in a patient, rather than understanding a person with a problem. The problem was labeled, while the person was overlooked" (Shectman 1973, p. 524). And, of course, as "Any good doctor knows . . . the patient's complaint is more extensive than his symptom, and the state of sickness more comprehensive than localized pain or dysfunction. As an old Jew put it . . . 'Doctor, my bowels are sluggish, my feet hurt, my heart jumps—and you know, Doctor, I myself don't feel so well either' " (Erikson 1964, p. 51).

But you cannot deny that the pseudopatients were undetected.

That was due more to a lack of carefully observing and carefully thinking than to an inability to distinguish faking patients from real ones.

What is your evidence for that?

Rosenhan himself reports that ". . . many real patients detected the pseudopatients. This fact in itself demonstrates that diagnosis can be valid and undercuts the conclusion that sanity cannot be differentiated from insanity. . . . Ironically, the patients thus exemplified the diagnostic work the staff failed to do. What the staff forgot was the necessity for eliciting and observing psychological functioning and not simply obtaining an account of it. In diagnosing a physical disease, the physician would not rely only on the patient's report of his symptoms. He might recommend that the patient enter a hospital for further study, just as the pseudopatients were advised, but the physician would also examine directly and utilize laboratory procedures to determine what hard evidence existed for the presence of the disease. He would compare these findings with the patient's account, and determine if the two corresponded. If not, he would then be forced to admit puzzlement and would realize that he would need to investigate further. A case in point in the history of psychiatry is the discovery of conversion reactions which manifested themselves in apparent dysfunctions which could not be linked to physical disease. Here the discontinuity led to a questioning attitude and further study. The staff, however, missed the glaring incongruity between the presenting complaint and the absence of correspondence in the pseudopatients' reports of their lives and their actual functioning in the hospital" (Shectman 1973, p. 524).

For me, ". . . the disconcerting occurrence is not that the pseudopatients were hospitalized, for to do otherwise [might have meant overlooking] . . . the possibility of severe disorganization implied in hearing voices. And it is not necessarily damning that they were not discharged immediately upon appearing to be functioning adequately, for [deeply disturbed people] . . . have been known to hear voices, only later to appear well [even though] . . . the disturbance persisted beneath the surface. Or, patients have been known to develop remissions" (Shectman 1973, p. 525). And there are ". . . well-known analogies in somatic medicine of effective malingering, of the elaborated so-called 'Münchausen Syndrome,' of the polysurgical addict who has succeeded in having numerous unnecessary operations performed upon himself, etc. Yet the fact that this can occur (and fool even the best) is nowhere taken to invalidate surgical diagnosis or the existence of true surgical illness, or to prove that it resides primarily in the surgeon's head and/or in his consequent willing propensity to label someone surgically ill" (Wallerstein 1973, p. 527). The element in Rosenhan's report which ". . . is disconcerting is that the discrepancy between the presenting symptom and the overall conduct of the pseudopatient was not seen; or, if recognized, it did not lead to a questioning, inquiring attitude in which remission was regarded as but one hypothesis among many to be systematically investigated. Rather, the explanation of remission was arrived at automatically and thereby foreclosed any true diagnostic work" (Shectman 1973, p. 525). For instance, one respondent to Rosenhan points out ". . . that not a single one of the diagnosticians seemed concerned with the possibility of an organic psychosis when faced with the sudden onset of auditory hallucinations in a previously well person; [there was a striking] . . . absence of the usual laboratory procedures designed to uncover toxic or organic central nervous system involvements, as well as the seeming absence of adequate psychiatric history taking, or social history from collateral interviews, or any felt indication for clinical psychological testing" (Wallerstein 1973, p. 528).

What else do you see this study as illustrating?

How data can be forced to fit preconceived conclusions. "Indeed, abuse of diagnosis followed misuse of it, for not only was remission mechanistically assumed, but the facts of the cases were unwittingly forced to fit what would be expected by a theory of schizophrenic reaction. For example, the pseudopatients' reports of relatively innocuous relationships with their parents were perceived as pathogenic ones so as to satisfy consistency with regard to what would be expected on the basis of the dynamics of schizophrenia. . . . But this problem is not new. Freud was concerned about the role of suggestion and how his patients could be unintentionally influenced to prove his ideas, leading to circularity rather than to discovery. Rapaport also worried about the possibility of 'smuggling in the confirmation through the interpretation.' Any scientist needs to be guided by where his data lead him, allowing—even watching—for his ideas to be disproved. Failure to do so indicts him as a scientist, but not the method of science, be it psychiatric diagnosis or laboratory experiment" (Shectman 1973, p. 525).

You do agree, then, that the study has much merit.

Definitely! "Rosenhan has performed a valuable service by dramatically showing how misused efforts to understand and help can be worse than useless; they can be outright harmful. But, again, this abuse is not intrinsic to diagnosis . . . and to believe that it is only obscures the point and fosters the incorrect [and unfortunate] belief that because some practices may be poor . . . [diagnosticians] should not practice" (Shectman 1973, p. 525).

That distinction is nice, but would you not agree that diagnosis is valuable only if treatments already exist to help the patient?

Not at all, because ". . . diagnosis in itself can lead to eventual treatment discoveries by virtue of its use of investigation, experimentation, and research. General paresis was differentiated . . . by the careful noting and describing of the symptom pattern by Bayle which led to its differentiation as a specific form of mental illness. Further diagnostic work by [many other people] . . . . led to the development of diagnostic procedures for determining involvement of the central nervous system and for the presence of spirochaetes in the blood stream. It was not until a century after Bayle's description that Ehrlich and Wagner-Jauregg developed the first treatment for paresis. Sound diagnosis ultimately led to the identification of causes and to the development of a specific treatment" (Shevrin & Shectman 1973, p. 465). Closer to psychiatry are the treatment implications that grew out of the Menninger Foundation's Psychotherapy Research Project; careful diagnostic work helped lead to a new understanding concerning the treatment of certain patients, especially those with borderline personality organizations (Kernberg 1975).

Our time is growing short, and I have left for last the objection that psychiatric diagnosis is anchored in an outdated and inappropriate way of thinking because of its tie to the medical model. Advocates of this viewpoint (Albee 1970; Patterson 1948; Szasz 1961) regard it as incorrect to look upon psychiatric disturbance according to a model so closely linked to physical disease. Like others, Chu and Trotter (1974), authors of a Nader report examining the mental health professions, imply that different levels of functioning are involved, i.e., physical-chemical versus psychological-social. Taken together, these advocates make the points (1) that it is philosophically inconsistent to mix such universes of discourse and account for behavior on one plane by positing explanations from another realm, and (2) that it hamstrings psychiatric advances by forcing things into an anachronistic and inappropriate "disease" model.

The argument you seem to be making is that psychological problems cannot be equated with diseases like pneumonia or cancer. However, that viewpoint assumes a dualistic orientation of psychological versus physiological, and clearly there is reason to question such a division. For me, it is more sound to think of the organism's unity (Engel 1968; Selye 1974) in which structural, chemical, emotional, ideational, perceptual, and interpersonal changes interact continuously with one another. From that standpoint, it would be illogical to talk about a diseased lung while ignoring the human being and his family who are altered by that disease; similarly, it would be just as illogical to talk about a neurosis while ignoring the altered breathing, muscular imbalances, and interpersonal vicissitudes that are an integral part of that person's "dis-ease." This viewpoint is consistent with Reich's (1949) emphasis on "character armoring" and concomitant physical alterations as a function of the psychiatric disturbance. Some of the newer therapies, which are espoused by physicians and nonphysicians alike, stress techniques that are designed to bring about psychological change through body manipulation (Alexander 1974; Rolf 1975).

I am glad you mention nonphysicians, because another objection is that ". . . the medical model . . . is seen as a weapon in the political warfare between physicians and other professionals. . . . Priority and status, according to this argument, are attributed to those who have society's sanction to 'practice medicine' . . ." (Shevrin & Shectman 1973, p. 466), in other words, society's sanction to diagnose. As a matter of fact, ". . . the Nader report on community mental health . . . shows how the perpetuation of the medical model in community mental health has completely vitiated the possibilities of the movement and perpetuated a fraud on the people in the interest of those same vested interests. Or to put it another way, the rich get psychiatrists, the middle class get social workers, and the poor get paraprofessionals, each according to their means" (Gottesfeld 1974, p. 310).

As you note, that argument rests on political-economic grounds, not scientific ones, which, of course, makes it no less important or heartfelt. However, to use your idea, it does mix realms of discourse and unfairly blackens the eye of diagnosis because it may be improperly used, ". . . as if the medical model [a form of the scientific method as applied to psychiatric disorder] . . . could be the [sole] property of any one group" (Shevrin & Shectman 1973, p. 466).*

---

* cf. Sarason & Ganzer (1968).

We have covered a lot of ground. And although I am still not convinced of your viewpoint and will remain a humanist, I am reminded of the advertising slogan which says you do not have to be Jewish to enjoy Levy's ryebread. Perhaps you do not have to be against diagnosis to be a humanist. Maybe diagnosticians can be humanists as well.

Kindly put. My thinking has been stirred by the cogent challenges you have presented.

You have given me much to think about, too. You have provoked much in me—in the second sense you referred to previously, of course!

References

ALBEE, G. W.: The Uncertain Future of Clinical Psychology. *Am. Psychol.* 25(12):1071–80, 1970.

ALEXANDER, F. M.: *The Resurrection of the Body.* New York: Dell, 1974.

BACK, K. W.: *Beyond Words: The Story of Sensitivity Training and the Encounter Movement.* New York: Russell Sage Foundation, 1972.

BAUER, HERBERT: To Diagnose or Not to Diagnose: A Naïve Inquiry. *Int. J. Group Psychother.* 21(4):470–75, 1971.

BECK, A. T.: Reliability of Psychiatric Diagnoses: 1. A Critique of Systematic Studies. *Am. J. Psychiatry* 119(3):210–16, 1962.

CHU, F. D. & TROTTER, SHARLAND: *The Madness Establishment: Ralph Nader's Study Group Report on the National Institute of Mental Health.* New York: Grossman Publishers, 1974.

COOPER, J. E. et al.: *Psychiatric Diagnosis in New York and London: A Comparative Study of Mental Hospital Admissions* (Maudsley Monographs No. 20). London: Oxford University Press, 1972.

Decision Reached on Wyatt: U. S. Court of Appeals Reaffirms Right to Treatment. *APA Monitor* 6(1):6, 1975.

ENGEL, G. L.: The Psychoanalytic Approach to Psychosomatic Medicine. In *Modern Psychoanalysis: New Directions and Perspectives,* Judd Marmor, ed., pp. 251–73. New York: Basic Books, 1968.

ERIKSON, E. H.: *Insight and Responsibility: Lectures on the Ethical Implications of Psychoanalytic Insight.* New York: Norton, 1964.

FREUD, SIGMUND (1927): The Future of an Illusion. *Standard Edition* 21:5–56, 1961.

GIBSON, R. W.: The Use of Financing to Control the Delivery of Services. *Psychiatr. Annals* 4(1):22–41, 1974.

GOTTESFELD, M. L.: On Accountability in Mental Health: Or The Institutional Model Is Alive and Well and Irresponsible. *Clin. Soc. Work J.* 2(4):307–11, 1974.

GOUGH, HARRISON: Some Reflections on the Meaning of Psychodiagnosis. *Am. Psychol.* 26(2):160–67, 1971.

GOVE, W. R. & FAIN, TERRY: The Stigma of Mental Hospitalization: An Attempt to Evaluate Its Consequences. *Arch. Gen. Psychiatry* 28(4):494–500, 1973.

HORWITZ, LEONARD: *Clinical Prediction in Psychotherapy.* New York: Jason Aronson, 1974.

KENDELL, R. E.: Psychiatric Diagnoses: A Study of How They Are Made. *Br. J. Psychiatry* 122(4):437–45, 1973.

KERNBERG, O. F.: *Borderline Conditions and Pathological Narcissism.* New York: Jason Aronson, 1975.

KREITMAN, N. *et al.*: The Reliability of Psychiatric Assessment: An Analysis. *J. Ment. Sci.* 107(450):887–908, 1961.

LAING, R. D.: *The Politics of the Family and Other Essays.* New York: Pantheon, 1969.

LEVINSON, D. J. *et al.*: Becoming a Patient. *Arch. Gen. Psychiatry* 17(4):385–406, 1967.

MANN, ABBY: *Judgment at Nuremberg.* New York: Signet, 1961.

MASLOW, A. H.: *The Psychology of Science: A Reconnaissance.* New York: Harper & Row, 1966.

McDONALD, MARGARET: Supreme Court Rules on Donaldson v. O'Connor. *Psychiatr. News* 10(14):1, 22–23, 1975.

MENNINGER, K. A.: Hope. *Menninger Perspective* 5(4):4–11, 1974–1975.

MENNINGER, K. A. *et al.*: *The Vital Balance.* New York: Viking, 1963.

OSTOW, MORTIMER: Letter to the Editor. *Science* 180(4084):360–61, 1973.

PASAMANICK, BENJAMIN *et al.*: Psychiatric Orientation and Its Relation to Diagnosis and Treatment in a Mental Hospital. *Am. J. Psychiatry* 116(2):127–32, 1959.

PATTERSON, C. H.: Is Psychotherapy Dependent Upon Diagnosis? *Am. Psychol.* 3(5):155–59, 1948.

PRUYSER, P. W.: The Beleaguered Individual: Images of Man in Clinical Practice. *Bull. Menninger Clin.* 37(5):433–50, 1973.

REICH, WILHELM: *Character-Analysis,* Ed. 3, T. P. Wolfe, trans. New York: Orgone Institute Press, 1949.

ROGERS, C. R.: *Client-Centered Therapy: Its Current Practice, Implications, and Theory.* Boston: Houghton Mifflin, 1951.

ROLF, I. P.: *The Structural Integration of Human Beings.* New York: Viking, 1975.

ROSENHAN, D. L.: On Being Sane in Insane Places. *Science* 179(4070):250–58, 1973.

SARASON, I. G. & GANZER, V. J.: Concerning the Medical Model. *Am. Psychol.* 23(7):507–10, 1968.

SELYE, HANS: *Stress Without Distress.* Philadelphia: Lippincott, 1974.

SHECTMAN, FREDERICK: On Being Misinformed by Misleading Arguments. *Bull. Menninger Clin.* 37(5):523–25, 1973.

SHEVRIN, HOWARD & SHECTMAN, FREDERICK: The Diagnostic Process in Psychiatric Evaluations. *Bull. Menninger Clin.* 37(5):451–94, 1973.

SOLZHENITSYN, A. I.: *The Gulag Archipelago, 1918–1956: An Experiment in Literary Investigation, I–II,* T. P. Whitney, trans. New York: Harper & Row, 1974.

STICKNEY, STONEWALL: Wyatt vs. Stickney: The Right to Treatment. *Psychiatr. Annals* 4(8):32–45, 1974.

STRAUSS, J. S.: Diagnostic Models and the Nature of Psychiatric Disorder. *Arch. Gen. Psychiatry* 29(4):445–49, 1973.

SULLIVAN, F. W.: Professional Standards Review Organizations: The Current Scene. *Am. J. Psychiatry* 131(12):1354–57, 1974.

SZASZ, T. S.: *The Myth of Mental Illness: Foundations of a Theory of Personal Conduct.* New York: Hoeber-Harper, 1961.

———: *The Manufacture of Madness: A Comparative Study of the Inquisition and the Mental Health Movement.* New York: Harper & Row, 1970.

———: *Ceremonial Chemistry: The Ritual Persecution of Drugs, Addicts, and Pushers.* Garden City, NY: Anchor Press, 1974.

WALLERSTEIN, R. S.: Discussion of Rosenhan's "On Being Sane in Insane Places." *Bull. Menninger Clin.* 37(5):526–30, 1973.

WEINER, I. B.: Does Psychodiagnosis Have a Future? *J. Pers. Assess.* 36(6):534–46, 1972.

WELCH, C. E.: PSRO's—Pros and Cons. *N. Engl. J. Med.* 290(23):1319–22, 1974.

Action,
The Diagnostic Focus

DANGER-SITUATIONS

The founding of the Menninger Clinic fifty years ago was an event of great significance in the history of psychiatry. Another great event coincided with this one, namely, Freud's writing "Inhibitions, Symptoms and Anxiety," and my presentation will be concerned with a reappraisal and further development of that text. It is, I think, especially fitting to take this as my task. For one thing, in this work Freud established fundamental, even revolutionary changes in the idea of diagnosis, especially as it pertains to the neuroses; for another, the theme of birth runs through that entire work, and we are together now to celebrate a birth.

Here I want to mention another birth, more exactly a rebirth. I am referring to the occasion of my coming to the Menninger Clinic in January, 1943, fresh out of college and a wide-eyed newcomer to the rich world Dr. Karl Menninger was creating here in Topeka. It was a world whose imprint has remained on all of my personal as well as professional activities. But, contrary to Freud's thesis in "Inhibitions, Symptoms and Anxiety" of birth as trauma, it was for me, and I believe for most others who worked and studied here, exactly the opposite of traumatic to be born or born again at the Menninger

---

* Professor of Psychology in Psychiatry, Cornell University Medical College, New York, New York.

Clinic. Even allowing for the rigorous training habits immediately imposed on me by my great teacher, David Rapaport, the Menninger Clinic was as much like a good womb as the outside world can be.

One will understand, therefore, how honored I was by the invitation to be the featured speaker at this birthday party, and also how I could not accept the invitation without the anxiety that inevitably accompanies a formal and emphatic recognition that in some important sense one has grown up. Whether inhibitions and symptoms were also a part of my response to this occasion, I shall leave to the reader to judge for himself or herself.

"Inhibitions, Symptoms and Anxiety" is the most modern of Freud's theoretical treatises. In this work, Freud systematically introduced a new way of looking at the neuroses and their clinical treatment—a way so true, so useful, and by now so familiar that one all too easily often underestimates its achievement. By formally defining danger-situations, arranging these situations chronologically, and aligning them with the various neuroses, he developed a new perspective on the treatment of the neuroses. In that perspective, one's therapeutic goal is to help the patient consciously recognize danger-situations and to understand how in his life history these situations evolved and persisted and the means that were adopted to cope with them. In this last respect, the patient's characteristic unconscious defensive activities are of particular significance.

In what follows I shall justify this appraisal of "Inhibitions, Symptoms and Anxiety" while sorting out some of the weaker parts of Freud's argument. In executing this project, I shall make extensive use of my own recent theoretical work (1976) on the new language for systematic psychoanalysis that I call *action language*. I shall arrive at a concept of anxiety and of all affects as an action or mode of action best rendered through the use of a family of verbs and adverbs. In light of this conception, I shall review the key terms of Freud's treatise and discuss other key terms such as *character traits*, *defenses*, and *diagnosis and therapy*.

Anxiety

Freud succinctly summarized the conclusion of his discussion on anxiety in the following words: "A danger-situation is a recognized, remembered, expected situation of helplessness" (p. 166). The sequence of danger-situations, following the traumatic situations of helplessness at birth and during early infantile periods of intense bodily need, are loss of object, loss of the object's love, castration, and superego condemnation. Anxiety is the appropriate response to danger-situations as it is to the initial traumatic situations. In danger-situations, however, the ego attempts to restrict the anxiety response and to use it as a signal for instigating its own defensive measures. Anxiety functions, then, as the motive for defense; more exactly, it is the ego's anticipation of a traumatic situation of which the preliminary anxiety reaction is a portent, together with the ego's function of avoiding unpleasure, that establishes the occasion of defense.

First of all it is important to decide just what kind of theory this is. One must say that it is a cognitive and experiential theory of anxiety; certainly it is no longer purely or primarily an energic theory like Freud's earlier theory according to which anxiety is transformed libido that has accumulated in excessive quantity. Helplessness is experience, a view of one's position in the world. The new theory forces the economic-quantitative approach very much into the background. Even though Freud continued to mention that anxiety is a biological discharge phenomenon, he also argued against this idea when he refuted Rank's theory of abreaction of the birth trauma through anxiety. He was similarly uncertain or ambivalent with respect to his earlier idea that it is countercathectic energy that is discharged in anxiety. He seemed no longer sure that this energic bookkeeping mattered. Of course Freud was not then, nor was he ever, prepared to give up his postulate of psychic energy and his metapsychological vantage point of psychoeconomics (witness his final addendum to "Inhibitions, Symptoms and Anxiety" on the subject of pain and the pain of mourning [pp. 169–72]). Still, what was new in this anxiety theory was basically its cognitive and experiential slant. The danger-situation, which is the occasion of anxiety, is what is recognized, remembered, and expected. It is defined by ego functions or, as I prefer to say, by the actions of recognizing, remembering, and anticipating.

At this point I should like to introduce a superordinate conception of danger-situations, one that encompasses this cognitive, experiential, ego-functional account. According to this conception, a danger-situation corresponds to an action taken by a person to define situations from a certain standpoint. This action is constituted by particular actions, such as recognizing, remembering, and anticipating. To call it an action may be troubling, for it is customary to think of action as overt motor behavior in or on the environment. One thinks of it this way both in ordinary language and within the psychoanalytic tradition of distinguishing thought and experience from action. Yet it is entirely legitimate to subsume the varieties of thinking and experience under action in that it is consistent with modern philosophical discussions of action. It is also consistent with some ideas that have always been implicit in the psychoanalytic theory of consciousness and ego functions. I am thinking, for instance, of the implicit idea that the mental qualities—consciousness, preconsciousness, and unconsciousness—are to be viewed as explainable activities in that they are features of the ego's shifting about of cathexes in keeping with its own interests. Thus, thinking in one or another mode of consciousness is something one does or refrains from doing.

Another such instance is the idea we hold of ego functions as being activated or suspended by the superordinate organizing function of the ego. Implied in this idea is the notion that an ego function, too, is something one does or refrains from doing. As psychoanalytic therapists we faithfully adhere to these ideas in our clinical work: We interpret why the patient has or has not seen, recalled, or anticipated something, and why the patient has or has not experienced it in a certain way.

Although an appreciation of Freud's forward leap does not depend on one's viewing it in terms of action language, I want to explain how the notion of situations, when carefully elucidated, is especially compatible with action language and even requires the development and adoption of some such language.

In Freud's new theory, everything turns on the concept of situation. As presented by Freud, the notion of situation implies several fundamental propositions that must be spelled out. On the most general level, the natural science language of forces, energies, mechanisms, and the like, is to be set aside in favor of a language devoted to meanings, for a situation is not an object or an environment or an ego function, but necessarily the individual version of reality that is currently understood and experienced by a person, especially un-consciously. How a person sees his or her circumstances and views himself or herself in relation to these circumstances is a technical concept of situation more useful than the ambiguous one of ordinary language.

It is true that Freud emphasized "psychical situations" earlier. For instance, in "Introductory Lectures on Psycho-Analysis" (1916) he discussed his method of rendering dreams intelligible, showing that they "have a sense," a meaning. But up to this point in the history of his theory-making, Freud had consistently treated meaning as phenomenon in a naive empiricist fashion; that is to say, that al-though Freud was always concerned with the further definition of meanings and the specification of the life histories of meanings, he consistently viewed the job of scientific psychoanalytic explanation as requiring one to take a further step of translating phenomena into mechanistic and organismic terms of metapsychology.

In his revised theory of anxiety, however, he was unself-con-sciously reversing the explanatory priorities by placing meaning at the center of his theory. But even his continuing energic account of anxiety and its regulation depended on one's first defining the mean-ingful situation, while his instinctual account of the origin of danger-situations could no longer be decisive. As he pointed out, instincts are not dangerous in and of themselves; they become the occasions of danger when they are defined as such by the child or adult.

Once we develop our explanations in a universe of meanings rather than forces, we cannot avoid viewing the person as the interpreter of circumstances and needs, that is, as the definer and assigner of meanings. Danger-situations are thus personal construc-tions, and whether or not a person constructs a danger-situation will depend on his or her conceptions and estimates of self relative to circumstance. It also follows that, strictly speaking, the earliest traumatic situations, starting with birth, are not situations at all in that they refer to prementational events: A newborn cannot con-ceive situations, and physiological stress or disequilibrium is not yet a situation. At that point in development one can speak of helpless-ness only from the standpoint of an objective, independent observer, and that was not at all what Freud was referring to.

One might wonder why I keep saying *person* rather than *ego* and I will discuss this later, especially in the following section on "Inhibition." One might also wonder if I am denying the place of the body and its maturation in psychoanalytic explanation. As psychoanalytically-oriented thinkers and therapists, we are quite at home with the idea that people construct their own situations, but we consider it under other names: *phase-specificity*, and *transference and resistance*. Phase-specificity refers of course to the fact that, at each stage of bodily maturation and development, the child will attribute meanings to self and circumstance appropriate to that stage. This observation puts us in the familiar clinical realm of oral meanings, anal meanings, phallic meanings, and genital meanings, and of the particular erotic and aggressive aims the person sets in terms of these psychosexual reference points. Today, we might add to this list separation-individuation conceived in bodily terms. But, historically, we can trace the idea of phase-specificity back to Freud's early emphasis on the delayed impacts of seduction during early childhood and the discovery of the anatomical difference between the sexes, and also on the dominance during childhood of early infantile sexual theories over enlightened sex education. A cardinal feature of the genetic approach of psychoanalysis is that bodily categorial principles play a great part in the child's construction of reality. These categorial principles are unconsciously carried forward into adult life. Psychosexual zones and modes shape the construction of situations.

The point of phase-specificity, then, is that situations are never given: The child and later the adult fashion and perpetuate situations and do so unconsciously as well as preconsciously and consciously, and always in terms of the bodily and developmental issues and the level of cognitive maturity that predominates at the time. In this sense a situation corresponds to an action. To say that the situation is defined, created, or constructed is to say that someone is doing something, i.e., engaging in action. A situation, of course, is not created out of whole cloth. From the dawn of mental activity, each person takes into account necessity and accident, but he or she can only do so in phase-specific and individually characteristic ways. However much one agrees with others in certain "objective" respects, and however limited and directed one may be by bodily

makeup, maturation, and the conditions and language of one's up-
bringing, one may still be viewed as authoring one's own life. Thus,
transference and resistance are ways the analysand takes into account the necessities and accidents of the treatment relationship. As
one patient said, "Any question you ask me makes me anxious: I
take it as a criticism."

I do not need to elaborate the point that our interpretations of
transference and resistance consistently demonstrate that the patient
is repetitively constructing his or her archaic versions of the treatment relationship. My thesis applies to more than the construction
of a situation. It applies as well to the actions of the person in the
situation thus defined. For an essential aspect of maintaining the
nonbehavioristic orientation of psychoanalysis, of its concern with
psychic reality or unconscious fantasy, is to remember always that
what to an outside observer might look like identical items of behavior may mean other things to different agents or to one agent at
different times. Here we come directly to the concept of action as
I am using it, and how it is integrally related to the concept of
situation.

Action refers to all behavior performed in a personally meaningful, purposive or goal-directed fashion and includes all the forms of
thinking and (as we shall see) feeling as well. Action does not imply
conscious awareness. It cannot be fully described by an independent
observer acting alone, for it is not exclusively or mainly a social-
psychological concept. For instance, unconsciously the same insult
may be an excremental action for one person, a castrating action for
another, and perhaps both for a third. Similarly, solving a puzzle
may be an action that also answers the question of where babies
come from or of how it is that women do not have penises. Or
solving a puzzle may be mental masturbation, or an action that helps
master wishes to be fed, or a step in the passing of an examination,
or several or all of these actions at once. We refer to this recognition of the variable and multiple meanings of specific actions as
their overdetermination, their multiple function, or simply their
psychic reality, all representing a metapsychological way of talking.
In effect, however, in elucidating these meanings or these multiple
actions implied by one action, we are giving psychoanalytic answers
to the questions, "What is this person doing?" and "Why is he or she

doing it and doing it just that way?" Psychoanalytically-oriented therapists are especially interested in certain definitions of actions, ones that convey the infantile erotic and aggressive sense in what the patient is doing and the infantile hazards and protective measures connected with this sense.

With this much understood about the technical notion of situations, we may return to the danger-situation specifically. I want to point out that the idea of a danger-situation and the idea of what one is doing in it or would like to do about it are correlative. Each implies the other. To say something about one is necessarily to say something about the other. For example, the danger-situation of castration exists when one views one's actual or conditional actions as the kind that will create that danger, e.g., actions of oedipal seduction and attacking the paternal phallus are both danger-creating actions. Therefore, if one is in a situation that clearly seems to threaten retaliatory mutilation or impairment of prowess, one will define one's actions accordingly: One's conception of them will be situation-bound; they will be intelligible only in terms of that situation. The castration anxiety of Little Hans is a case in point. We are used to dealing with stimulus-response relations in this way, that is, to see in each case that the stimulus has already been defined in ways implying the response to be made to it.

Another important correlative of action and situation is affect which enters into the experiential conception of danger-situations. Throughout the ages and throughout the history of psychoanalytic theory, affects have been treated nominatively, i.e., as independent entities with which the person, ego, or self must cope. Our ordinary language is rich in words, phrases, and figures of speech that teach us to think this way about affects and steadily reinforce our doing so. We think of affects as coming and going; we think they overwhelm us or support us or enrich us; we believe we hold them in, that we get rid of them in catharsis, that they get under our skin, and so on. Even when they are viewed metapsychologically, as the quantitative aspect of instinctual drives whereby they seem to be established as aspects of ourselves, these aspects are still often said to impinge on the ego and thus to be encountered as something other than ourselves. They remain entities we must contend with or independent processes we must suffer or enjoy as the case may be. Especially in the case of moods and pathological emotional states, such as depression, we, equally as lay people and analytic observers, ordinarily view affects in this anthropomorphic and disclaimed way. It is, I should emphasize, a way that sets up the person as inherently passive and reactive in relation to affects.

But I think it is not necessary and no longer helpful to think this way, for this view of the matter is logically flawed and does not conform closely to essential aspects of psychoanalytic interpretation. In both respects, affects may be better regarded as defining phenomena of the self or ego or person. For this reason analytic therapists do not hesitate to raise questions as to why someone feels a certain way and why he or she even makes sure to feel that way or not feel that way. By doing so, these therapists reject the conventional disclaiming separation of the person from his or her affects.

For example, therapists view neurotic depression as an aspect of the person's actions, and thus they follow the clinical explanation Freud advanced concerning mourning and melancholia. Quite apart from Freud's extensive and unproductive psychoeconomic speculation about the painfulness of the depressive affects, speculations he then regarded as his scientific metapsychological account of these matters, he was advancing an account of mourning and melancholia that tells what people are doing when they mourn or are depressed: They introject and punish other persons whom they regard ambivalently, meanwhile sparing them from direct attacks; or they slowly face up to the reality of an actual loss and do so by reviewing and reliving the multitude of memories of the relationship that has, in the commonsense view, ended. In these activities, they regard themselves reproachfully or hatefully, or they remember sadly in order to face facts and go on living. For better or worse, they conduct their lives painfully. According to this clinical explanation, depression is not an entity to be encountered; like diplomacy, it is war conducted by other means, or else it is reality testing conducted reluctantly and miserably, but usefully as well.

I have just used a number of adverbs to characterize the affective states of the mourning and melancholic person—*reproachfully, hatefully, sadly, painfully,* etc. To return again to the danger-situations outlined in "Inhibitions, Symptoms and Anxiety," which is to return to the neuroses and specifically to anxiety, I would say that Freud was necessarily talking about the person considering certain situations anxiously; he could not be referring to the entity, *anxiety*, passively encountered by a person or ego. I say this for several reasons. My first reason is to modify my previous description of ordinary and psychoanalytic language, for it is not the case that we invariably designate affects as entities not of the self. The fact is that we also have a large and well-used stock of verbs and adverbs by which to designate affects. We say "to love" and "lovingly," "to hate" and "hatefully," "to fear" and "fearfully," or that one climbs "anxiously," reminisces "nostalgically," loves "passionately," etc. In these locutions we specify affects not as disclaimed entities, but as personal actions or modes of action. It is this aspect of our thinking about affects that may be directly incorporated into action language. In action language there are no personified and autonomous mental entities, emotional or otherwise. Nouns and adjectives give way to verbs and adverbs. Far from being merely a stylistic change, action language establishes an entirely different view of existence or of what it is to be a person. Persons are no longer regarded as the arenas and resultants of mental forces; they are their own actions and the modes in which they perform these actions. Their identities reside in what can be said in a general way about their actions. Action is not restricted to overt behavior or conscious thinking.

My stressing this conception of situations and actions constructed anxiously, and thus the verbal and adverbial version of affects, is not so far as it might seem from Freud's theory of psychic structure. Freud's new anxiety theory sets forth the ego as the seat of anxiety. Not only does he argue that the ego perceives the anxiety and uses it as a signal, he also argues that the ego defines the danger-situation to begin with. In the structural theory, what else but the ego would and could recognize, remember, and expect situations of any kind? It is the ego, that coherent group of functions, that does so. Anxiety is thus an activity of the ego or, in other words, acting anxiously is a defining feature of what we call the ego (the id and superego do not, by definition, act anxiously). In this way Freud established an active conception of anxiety in keeping with his structural theory.

My stressing the verbal and adverbial conception of danger-situations ties in with my assertion that affect is a correlative of action and situation. For if affect or emotion may be stated as action, and if action and situation are correlatives, then affect is a correlative of both. The meaning of this statement is quite in line with the usual clinical way of understanding affects.

How do we know that someone is in a danger-situation? Of course people may tell us that they feel unaccountably frightened or apprehensive, but we do not have to depend on their report, and anyway they may be pretending or trying to mislead us. Also, people are often unaware of anxiety signals. When, according to usual criteria, a person is fleeing or getting ready to flee from a scene, or reports such action in a convincingly agitated fashion, or acts in ways that imply fleeing, or perhaps shows some of the familiar physiological signs that accompany flight reactions, it is safe to infer that the person is in a danger-situation. And when, objectively, there seems to be no danger to flee from, we assume we are dealing with an unconsciously defined danger-situation and with "neurotic anxiety." For example, the person dreads a friendly embrace or an open street or an ordinary horse; the action and mode of action implies the danger-situation. The action may be an emotion-action ("to fear"), or the mode might be an emotion-mode ("to run fearfully").

Danger-situations can be identified in other ways. When we observe a person rigidly avoiding certain objectively innocuous situations, we infer that the person unconsciously views them as danger-situations; emotion-actions and emotion-modes need not be in evidence. If our inference is correct, these "anxious" actions and modes will be in evidence whenever that person is compelled to enter or stay in that situation—for instance, forced to go out in the street, or to part from mother in the nursery school, or to talk about a certain topic. Thus, how a person acts or what a person does overtly that he has done only privately before can be used to establish the existence of a danger-situation. On this basis the therapist can say to a patient: "You are afraid even though you deny it. You wouldn't be acting defensively if you weren't afraid." Or the therapist can say, "You would be frightened to think so and even more frightened to do so."

If anxiety, danger-situation, and action are correlatives, the idea that the ego perceives a danger-situation and then gives itself a signal of anxiety is tautological. There could be no danger-situation unless one were acting anxiously or clearly avoiding doing so; that is one way we know a danger-situation exists. Also one would not act anxiously unless there was a danger-situation. We are dealing here not with causes but with codefining features of a psychological event. To say that the ego perceives anxiety would be a categorical mistake, for defining situations anxiously is one of the things we refer to by the abstract term ego. Any other understanding of these terms entails all the difficulties of the James-Lange theory of emotion according to which the behavioral response precedes the psychological defining of an affect.

The theory of signal anxiety is also a problem-laden theory because of its commitment to a metapsychology with its language of energy, structure, function, and mechanism. It is true that people often consciously deny being in danger-situations and only admit it to themselves after they notice signs of agitation; but rather than establish a case for the anxiety signal, these observations show that people sometimes revise their defensive orientations in the light of new, even if unwelcome, evidence, that is, new developments in their danger-situations.

The correlative action theory, in contrast, escapes these problems. Moreover, we use it in commonsense fashion in our clinical interpretations, though perhaps we do not realize we are doing so because our metapsychology stands in the way. I for one feel better because I no longer have to try and make sense of the proposition that the ego signals itself: I cannot picture it except as the ego rushing from one end of a telephone line to the other in time to catch its own message.

Inhibition

Inhibition must be approached as we now approach anxiety, that is, it must be rendered as a verb, "to inhibit," or an adverb, "inhibitedly." According to Freud, the reason for inhibiting or acting inhibitedly is to prevent the stimulation and experience of anxiety by avoiding a danger-situation. What is to be inhibited or done in an inhibited fashion may be a specific action, such as showing interest in another person, or a whole class of actions and modes of action that, metapsychologically, might be subsumed under one or more of the ego functions involved in performing certain tasks skillfully or at all. Further, one's neurotically inhibiting specific actions or classes of actions in order to avoid a danger-situation is to be explained, according to Freud, in the following manner: Unconsciously, the actions and modes in question gratify impulses, the expression or conscious experience of which it is anticipated would establish a danger-situation. Thus, only manifestly is it ever an action or class of actions that one inhibits. Ultimately, according to Freud, one aims to inhibit a latent impulse or group of impulses. We should, therefore, pause at this point to examine the fundamental psychoanalytic concept of impulse from the vantage point of the rules of action language. Much of the new anxiety theory turns on this concept.

A cornerstone of the structural and dynamic theory of psychoanalysis is that conflict exists primarily between the ego and the impulses of the id. To make this statement is not to deny the great importance of the ego's internal conflicts and its conflicts with the superego, nor is it to deny that these conflicts must be clarified in their own terms: It is to recognize that (1) id-ego conflicts are almost always implied in these other conflicts, and (2) the conceptualization of these other conflicts follows the lines laid down for speaking of the antagonistic relations of id and ego.

What, then, is an impulse in the terms of action language? More exactly, how shall we speak of an impulse verbally and adverbally? An impulse is an action one wishes to perform but refrains from performing. It is a conditional action, something one would do if it seemed safe enough to do so, or, if not a conditional action, then a conditional mode of action, such as doing something cruelly or seductively. We know, for instance, that almost all people regard certain actions as never safe enough to perform, whether in fact or in conscious imagining; among these are incestuous, parricidal, and cannibalistic actions. These actions remain unthinkable, where "unthinkable" can only mean consciously unthinkable, for we know that, unconsciously, people must wish to perform the actions on which they impose taboos. These actions remain forever conditional actions.

If an impulse is viewed as an action one wishes to take but refrains from taking, then the experience of impulse can only be a manifestation of already existing conflict; it is the conflict between doing and refraining. Otherwise the person would simply perform the action in question. This conclusion, although I have not stated it metapsychologically, is in line with what Freud called functioning according to the primary process that characterizes the id, imposing no delay on discharge and executing no experimental action in thought prior to discharge or, as I would say, prior to immediate action. Thus, what we or our patients call inhibiting impulses amounts to *further* inhibiting of actions or further refraining from performing them, however much one continues to wish to perform them. In this light, when we consider a manifest instance of inhibiting, we are dealing with someone's refraining from actions that he or she merely designates as impulse expressions. Metapsychologically, we would say that the inhibited ego function has been libidinized or aggressivized; whereas in action language we would say that, unconsciously, what one inhibits amounts to some sort of aggressive or erotic action or mode of action.

Although at this point we are far from the metapsychological way of conceptualizing id, instinctual drives, and psychic energies, we are, I submit, at the very center of clinical interpretation. For explicitly or implicitly we center our interpretations on actions and conditional actions and their modes, and especially on their unconsciously implied meanings. Clinically, we also center interpretations on the defensive disclaimings patients engage in when they speak of struggling with their impulses, for we understand that by putting it that way they are excluding these impulses from their own ideas of themselves and are disavowing having any responsible part in them. In this respect, the therapist tries to show the patient that he would like to perform the actions in question but does not dare do so and refrains from doing so. The therapist also tries to establish why the impulse is present and how the inhibition is accomplished. Thereby the therapist brings home to the patient that he (the patient) is as implicated in the impulse as in the effort to control or repudiate it.

In action language, one does not struggle with one's id or one's unconscious as autonomous entities; one struggles with oneself, or, better, one tries to choose between paradoxical actions or somehow combine them or go on doing both.

If the words I have just used are not the very words of these interpretations, they convey their sense. During the progress of an analytic therapy one can note the ever-increasing presentation of oneself as the agent of one's current life. Less and less do patients present themselves as lived by impulses, emotions, defenses, or conflicts; more and more do they present themselves as the authors of their existence. For even when all the necessities or terrible happenings of their past and present existences have been taken into account, patients come to realize how much has always depended on what they have made of these factors, whether they be family constellations, traumas, infirmities, losses, or sexual anatomy. In fact, it is only on the basis of this arduously achieved realization that patients can sort out their personal irrational constructions from rationally appraised necessity or accident—sorting out, for example, unwarranted ideas of unworthiness from more objectively considered parental neglect that occasioned them. To go further into the theoretical fates of drives, energies, motives, external reality, and determinism in the scheme of action language would require a discussion too lengthy for this paper. I have attempted to deal with these crucial issues in a number of other discussions (1976).

One final consideration about inhibition. I prefer to say *refraining* from taking certain actions rather than *inhibiting* them because refraining is more consistent with action language. To say inhibiting is to imply the existence of both agentless independent forces and some concept of "inside" in which these forces can be contained. Both of these implications can be shown to be logically problematic even within the traditional metapsychological framework. That they are inconsistent with the requirements of a systematic action language should by now be evident.

Symptoms

In viewing symptoms as actions, the first job is to realize that what we are used to calling overdetermination or multiple determination and multiple function of symptoms may now be designated as complex actions. In clinical interpretation we attempt to make symptoms intelligible; we do so by progressively bringing them into the realm of claimed or acknowledged actions that the patient is performing. Specifically, we try to ascertain in what ways symptoms are wishful activities such as enactments of primal scenes, in what ways they are self-punitive activities such as enactments of castration, and in what ways they are defensive, organizing, and adaptive activities. Thereby we take into account their so-called multiple function with respect to id, superego, and ego, respectively. Also in each of these structural respects we attempt to identify the many different wishful, self-punitive, and other meanings they carry; thereby we take into account their so-called overdetermination.

In working out these interpretations we progressively establish the following point: Far from being afflictions visited on the hapless patient which must be cured, neurotic symptoms are actions in which the patient has a definite stake and is most reluctant to give up. The stake and the reluctance are intimately related to the patient's unconsciously expecting to be left exposed to those danger-situations which the symptom was designed to forestall in the first place.

It is important to recall in this connection that much of the analysis of symptoms is not conducted explicitly in relation to them; rather, it is conducted in terms of manifest content far afield from them, perhaps in relation to certain neurotic character traits or certain features of the transference and resistance. It is also important to recall that it is not unusual for patients to mention, late in the treatment, the alleviation or disappearance of certain symptoms that have not figured prominently in the analysis and may never have been mentioned at all. These symptoms include headaches, constipation, dysmenorrhea, gastric distress, and minor phobias and compulsions. The significance of these clinical observations lies in their close connection with the analysis of danger-situations, for wherever and however the analysis of chronic, characteristic danger-situations has been successful, the patient's stake in maintaining symptoms will have been diminished or eliminated. The patient will no longer have good and sufficient reason to act symptomatically or to act in ways that provoke or aggravate the physical aspects of his disturbances. Moreover, even when we take up symptoms directly, we find it especially useful in working out our interpretations of them to follow their exacerbations and alleviations; we do so on the assumption that these changes correspond to the waxing and waning of the danger-situations for which they have been designed and so point to the constituents of danger. The case is the same when we analyze defenses; we depend on their diminution and intensification, their flux; for when they remain static, we are left in a poor position to discover their specific point and are in no position at all to make clear that they are actions, that they have reasons, and so are intelligible and modifiable after all.

Character Traits

In action terms one would speak of neurotic character traits as one would speak of inhibitions and symptoms, that is, as complex actions. They can be analyzed insofar as they show the flux I referred to in discussing symptoms. They are chronic features of the patient's existence. Typically they extend back to early childhood, even though their manifest form may not have been consolidated until adolescence. They imply chronic danger-situations. The more disabling or disruptive they are, the more drastic or imminent the dangers they imply. What I chiefly want to emphasize is that, in thinking of them as traits, we commit ourselves to viewing them as properties one possesses, like facial features; whereas in thinking of them as actions and modes of action, we more usefully regard them as things one does consistently with reference to unconsciously defined and continuously maintained danger-situations.

Defenses

The great advance Freud made in "Inhibitions, Symptoms and Anxiety" with respect to defenses was not sorting out repression as merely one mechanism of defense among others, although to be sure this contribution was an advance. More important, he leaped far ahead of himself in his mode of conceptualizing by interpreting mechanisms as expressions of unconscious fantasy, that is, as meaningful or personal actions. He did this in his discussion of the relation in the obsessional disorders between isolation and touching and between undoing and anal blowing away. By analyzing the unconscious fantasy or the psychic reality of the defensive activity, Freud was able to say more fully and with more therapeutic effect what the obsessional patient does when engaging in isolating or undoing. In this respect the notion of a mechanism of the ego gave way implicitly to the notion of the person as agent—the right step for Freud to take in a treatise devoted to danger-situations. If touching becomes dangerous because of its anal-masturbatory significance, and if, unconsciously, thoughts and affects have come to be regarded concretely as anal-masturbatory substances or objects that are dangerously assaultive and seductive in themselves or that may be used in one of those manners, then the thing for one to do is to refrain from touching—at least one should refrain from touching in those areas of one's life where it would be most dangerous to touch at all. As we know, even thoughts, words, or letters might have to be kept from touching.

The regression that brings about this anal-masturbatory concern with touching is a regression from the oedipal danger-situation to an earlier anal danger-situation. In this connection Freud referred to the regressively debased Oedipus complex of the obsessional neurotic. And if the regression moves, as he said, to a point of fixation, then it is implied that certain anal-masturbatory danger-situations have always figured significantly in the obsessional patient's actions even though less so before the neurotic regression. But here Freud referred mechanistically to a regression to old channels of discharge.

It seems that Freud was not ready to recognize the nature and the extent of the forward leap I have been describing and so did not draw its implications. In his treatise, he neither analyzed the unconscious fantasies involved in each of the defenses nor appreciated that he had embarked on an inherently nonmechanistic course of conceptualization. Otto Fenichel (1941), while shrewdly emphasizing defense as personal activity, also did not make the most of this advance. It remained for Melanie Klein and others working with her to capitalize on Freud's great advance. They did so by insisting that all mechanisms be analyzed in terms of unconscious fantasy. However, they have interwoven this illuminating development with elaborations of metapsychology that are even more problematic than Freud's. Thus, in my view, they took the wrong turn and missed the opportunity of developing a unitary theory in terms of unconscious fantasy.

Diagnosis and Therapy

The implications of the preceding discussion for the idea we hold of diagnosis and therapy should be apparent by now. The words *diagnosis* and *therapy* are not problematic for action language—the one means "to distinguish" and the other "to serve," and we make such distinctions and render such service. It is the usual contexts of these words that are problematic.

We say we diagnose psychopathology; however, by the word *pathology* we refer to that which one suffers, thereby implying passivity and affliction. The word *patient* makes the same reference and has the same implications, and the word *symptom* means anything that has befallen one—again, the same view of things. But what Freud began to establish clearly in "Inhibitions, Symptoms and Anxiety," even though he did not systematically develop it, is the proposition that it is wrong to think that a neurosis befalls one. A neurosis is created and arranged and protected. It is, correlatively, the construction of danger-situations and the construction of emotional actions to take in these situations. Consequently, the diagnosis of neurosis is the diagnosis of the actions we are used to calling symptoms, neurotic character traits, impulses, defenses, affects, and functions.

If by a diagnosis we refer to what someone is doing, then we may designate a psychoanalytic therapy in comparable action terms. In the case of neurosis, the service we render is not really the cure of pathology. Rather, it consists of clarifying what the "patient" is doing, and to make sense of it in terms of unconsciously defined danger-situations. Then, by sorting out the past from the present and the imagined from the actual, the patient's sense of danger is diminished and he or she can open as well as reopen the possibilities of action. Increasingly during this process, the patient will present apparent demonic forces and unyielding structures as personal actions and begin to live his or her life less painfully, apprehensively, self-deceptively, and unintelligibly. The patient will construct other and better situations to live in and will do so with an enhanced and more rational sense of personal responsibility. The "cure" will be this personal transformation. For this reason we may not claim a "cure" when it is a matter only of the disappearance of symptoms, but we may do so in the face of some remaining symptoms despite the jeers and irrelevant statistics of the mechanistic behaviorists who deny the world of human action altogether.

In conclusion I want to say that the etymological implications of pathology, patient, and symptom apply to certain aspects of constitutional problems and hardships suffered by infants and young children—the factors that independently predispose them toward constructing certain worlds as against others. But one must question whether we could ever "cure" these predispositions and whether it even makes sense to think of them as something to which the word cure could rightly be applied—as though it would make sense to speak of curing history.

References

FENICHEL, OTTO: *Problems of Psychoanalytic Technique.* New York: Psychoanalytic Quarterly, 1941.

FREUD, SIGMUND (1916): Introductory Lectures on Psycho-Analysis: Parts I & II. *Standard Edition* 15:1–239, 1961.

———— (1926): Inhibitions, Symptoms and Anxiety. *Standard Edition* 20:87–175, 1959.

SCHAFER, ROY: *A New Language for Psychoanalysis.* New Haven: Yale University Press, 1976.

The Varying Scopes
Of Psychiatric Diagnosis

REFLECTIONS ON THE DIAGNOSTIC PROCESS BY A CLINICAL TEAM

JORGE DE LA TORRE, M.D.,* ANN APPELBAUM, M.D.,†
DORIS JANE CHEDIAK, M.S.W.,‡ WILLIAM H. SMITH, Ph.D.§

Introduction

In the Menninger tradition, the diagnostic process is not seen as an activity to be accomplished with maximum expediency, nor is the diagnostic team organized to give comfort to its individual members. Diagnosis is, rather, seen as a serious, exacting, exciting, and often rewarding and frequently courageous enterprise. The team is

* Director, Baylor Psychiatric Clinic; Faculty Member, Department of Psychiatry, Baylor College of Medicine and Houston/Galveston Psychoanalytic Institute, Houston, Texas. Formerly, Director of Diagnostic Service, C. F. Menninger Memorial Hospital, Topeka, Kansas. Dr. de la Torre organized and chaired this presentation and also discussed the contributions of the team consultant.

† Staff Psychiatrist, The Menninger Foundation; Faculty Member and Co-ordinator, Second-Year Residency Program, the Menninger School of Psychiatry; Instructor, Topeka Institute for Psychoanalysis.

‡ Private practice, Oklahoma City, Oklahoma. Formerly, Staff Member, Social Work Department, The Menninger Foundation, Topeka, Kansas.

§ Supervisor of Individual Psychotherapy in the Adult Psychotherapy Department, and Faculty Member in the Postdoctoral Training Program in Clinical Psychology, The Menninger Foundation; Chairman of the Curriculum Committee and Faculty Member, the Menninger School of Psychiatry, Topeka, Kansas.

careful not to slip into sterile or fanciful abstractions, but is always geared to one final product: improvement of the patient's condition.

In such a framework of tradition and practice, the psychiatric team participants are not substitutes for the functions of an ideal physician. Its members are skilled practitioners in their own right with original contributions to make to the diagnosis and treatment of psychiatric patients. In the general enthusiasm for psychiatric teams that arose in hospitals during the past decade, some of the principles and aims of multidisciplinary work may have become obscured. We would like to discuss these principles from the vantage point of the practitioners. Although the composition of a team varies according to its specific aim (frequently it will include nurses, activity therapists, psychiatric aides, teachers, or speech therapists), because of the time limit for this presentation we have confined ourselves to three distinct practitioners: a psychiatrist (Ann Appelbaum), a clinical psychologist (William Smith), and a psychiatric social worker (Doris Jane Chediak).

Clinical practice has given us strong convictions regarding the importance of a multidimensional view of a patient's functioning. Different perspectives with different observations and inferences yield several partial views of the patient which, when superimposed, give depth to the diagnostic image. All diagnostic work, moreover, has a longitudinal dimension representing the patient's history and a cross-sectional one representing the here and now that emerges during the examinations. If the diagnostic team is to operate as one articulate whole, functional cohesiveness with autonomy of units that share a common goal becomes necessary. The prerequisites for such a team include:

1. *Professional particularity*: Each member is to have a conviction about the worth of his professional work achieved through the maturation derived from training in his discipline. The opposite of professional particularity is professional diffusion, in which all members of the team try to be "accessory psychiatrists."

2. *Autonomy of diagnostic skills and tools*: Each member must feel comfortable and secure in using those particular skills and tools he knows best in such a way as to avoid competitive duplication.

3. *Role differentiation*: Each member must have a given position toward the diagnostic task, one member focusing on the
   intrapsychic functioning of the patient, others being particularly
   alert to the interpersonal or intrafamilial functioning, etc. The
   opposite of role differentiation is role homogenization.
4. *Ability to disagree*: Team members must maintain a climate
   of professional inquiry rather than slip into a stereotyped
   hierarchy leading to fearful acquiescence.
5. *Mutual respect*: This qualitative factor is based on regard for
   individual competence, with reciprocal opportunities to evaluate each other's contributions, instead of idealizing one member on the basis of his professional background.
6. *Group congruence*: The team upholds a coincidence in purposes that sustains rewarding working relationships; it resists
   malignant group dynamics.
7. *A common theoretical frame of reference*: This stance allows
   the team to pursue in depth certain inferences. Without such
   a frame of reference the team's work may be annulled by the
   disparity of theoretical premises.
8. *Supportive administrative structure*: Without administrative
   support all the previous *desiderata* become inoperative. The
   best clinical team will be rendered ineffectual if the administrative structure in which it operates does not take agreeable notice
   of its work, provide the necessary support, coordinate the
   work, make available the time, etc.

In order to reflect on the diagnostic process as we conduct it in
our daily work,* we have chosen a particular patient with whom we
worked to demonstrate how clinical team members, representing
different disciplines, actually engage each other. The case is not
striking or unusual; on the contrary, it comes close to what most
clinicians encounter in their practice. That, we feel, is precisely its
didactic strength.

---

* A diagnostic evaluation consists of daily interviews with a psychiatrist
while the patient's relative is seen by a psychiatric social worker. In addition,
a full battery of psychological testing, physical and neurological examination,
and laboratory and X-ray tests are also conducted. The whole process typically
lasts between one and two weeks.

The Team Psychiatrist

At the beginning of the presentation, we hinted at the rewards of diagnostic team work. This case is somewhat exceptional in that the patient, Sally F., offered a spontaneous, grateful, and complimentary follow-up. A few weeks after her return home from her diagnostic evaluation, she wrote the following letter:

Dear Doctor:
  I've been getting along very well since I got home two weeks ago. . . . I haven't felt nervous or depressed at all. I'm still having headaches, but I haven't had any severe ones and the ones I have had have been controlled pretty well by the medicine you gave me. Everything seems to be better. . . . My husband joined the church the Sunday after we got home, and for the first time religion plays a significant part in our lives. Believe me, it helps. I have already found a good part-time job which I will start next week. I bought a new sewing machine that will do almost anything, and I'm increasing my church participation and Bible study. Those things, with all I have been doing in spite of the headaches, should keep me busy enough that I won't have time to think about emotional things. Thank you again for what all of you did for my husband and me. I feel the trip was very profitable to both of us. I'll appreciate what you can do in helping to arrange for the further treatment you suggested for me here at home.

When the woman who wrote the letter first corresponded with us, she was so desperate after twelve years of a disabling illness that she wanted to move to Topeka from a distant state and put herself entirely in our hands. Her initial letter was a clear, well-organized account of unremitting daily headaches, punctuated with periods of severe anxiety, depression, fatigue, and emotional strain. She started each day by taking three or four Darvon capsules which she repeated every four hours with Bufferin in between. In the late afternoon she would rest and take Codeine without ever being relieved entirely of her pain. She had consulted many physicians. Ten years before she wrote to us she underwent an extensive neurological work-up including bilateral carotid angiograms and a spinal fluid examination which disclosed no neurological disturbance. At that time out-patient psychiatric treatment had been attempted for about six months followed by six weeks of hospitalization and electroshock treatment. But her condition remained unchanged.

During the ensuing decade, various tranquilizers in various dosages were tried. She had a thorough examination at the Mayo Clinic, where the headaches were attributed to muscle spasm and under-lying emotional conflicts. By the time she contacted us, she was having excruciating, continuous headaches and thought she was losing her mind. She was taking 200 mg. of Mellaril daily to which she had added 200 mg. of Sinequan, in addition to Elavil, Dalmane, Premarin, thyroid, and iron.

In response to this woman's request for help, we asked that she and her husband participate with a diagnostic team in a two-week study of the problem. In advance of their coming to Topeka, we asked each of them to fill out a packet of self-administered tests, a task requiring about two hours of concentrated independent effort. We also asked them to contact the physicians who had previously treated Mrs. F. for their reports. The message conveyed by these requirements is a significant one: "A group of us will set aside two weeks to work intensively with you; but at the same time we expect you to work intensively with us. You are not just a sick person who will 'go through the clinic' like a piece of faulty merchandise on a conveyor belt, but rather you and your family will be active par-ticipants in a search for understanding." We set a tone of serious dedication, telling the patient and her husband that business and family life must be interrupted for a period of total devotion to un-raveling the problem. In this case, as in many others, the impact of this preliminary phase of the study was such as to bring about a decrease of symptoms, a response which reflects in part hopefulness, and in part a shift of focus from suffering to working.

Before the patient arrived, the diagnostic team assembled for a brief conference to study the self-administered tests and other data. As one might imagine, the psychiatrist felt dubious about being able to help this chronically ill woman, the intractability of whose symp-toms might represent, among other things, a wish to control and defeat those who wish to help her. Perhaps the unusual clarity and articulateness of her initial letter reflected a struggle to contain an impending disorganization. If so, the study might upset her balance, and lead to referral for hospitalization—and these people were of modest means and probably could not afford a long and costly hospital treatment. Indeed they were making a considerable financial sacrifice to come to Topeka for this outpatient examination. Would the psychiatrist's work make this sacrifice worthwhile? Would this psychiatrist prove to be as impotent as all her previous doctors had been? The team consultant helped make these trepidations explicit, so the team members could support one another in facing the challenge and the possible disappointments that lay ahead.

A solitary psychiatrist, functioning without the emotional and intellectual nourishment of a sentient group, would find it hard to contain, tolerate, and examine the human pain being brought for diagnostic study, and to deal with feelings of anticipatory discouragement and self-doubt. Such feelings are mitigated in the kind of diagnostic study described here by the knowledge that the task is a time-limited one. It is easier to sustain attitudes of alertness, optimism, and concern—just as it is easier to be brave in the face of physical pain—when an end-point is established in advance.

The diagnostic study began on a Monday morning. The psychiatrist and the social worker met with the patient and her husband for an hour to define the problem, clarify the expectations of the clients about the study, and outline the procedure. Over the next two days the psychiatrist met twice with the patient, and the social worker met twice with the husband. Meanwhile four hours of psychological testing were scheduled. A complete physical examination, a neurological examination, and a full battery of laboratory tests were carried out.

On the third day of the study, the psychologist, social worker, and psychiatrist met with the team consultant to compare notes. The psychiatrist felt frustrated and inadequate: In the interviews, the patient had expressed high expectations of being cured and a willingness to do anything asked of her, while at the same time she demonstrated her distrust of the psychiatrist and her doubt that she could be helped. When the psychiatrist invited the patient to reflect upon possible connections between these attitudes, events of the past, and current symptoms, she talked endlessly about how unbearable her headaches had made her life. She listed the famous doctors and clinics she had consulted and the variety of treatment regimens she had undertaken without benefit. She spoke with evident satisfaction of how she had come to be "her own doctor" by learning to combine different medications so as to get better results than any of her physicians had been able to produce.

The psychologist shed light on the difficulties the psychiatrist was experiencing: He had found in this highly intelligent woman difficulties in attention and concentration against which she struggled by maintaining an appearance of composed detachment. The testing had uncovered her propensity for delusional reasoning, and her difficulty in distinguishing between inner and outer aspects of reality. She was nearly overwhelmed by anxiety and depression to the point of experiencing depersonalization (which was what she meant by "losing her mind"). Her doubts about the psychiatrist's capacity to help her represented her deep feelings of helplessness and needfulness, which made her experience others as also helpless, immobilized, and unresponsive. Meanwhile the social worker had found the husband psychologically naive but genuinely interested in his wife, committed to her welfare, and able to keep his own balance in the midst of the great frustrations in his marriage. Putting all this information together, the team developed a working hypothesis: The psychiatrist's effort to move Mrs. F. toward insight had made the patient feel psychologically endangered. What she needed from the psychiatrist was a more accepting and supportive attitude and help in organizing her thoughts and sorting out her confusion.

In the ensuing eight hours with the psychiatrist, Mrs. F. rapidly responded to the more supportive atmosphere of the interviews by gradually becoming more tolerant of her inner experiences, putting her introspection at the service of improving her condition rather than of contending with her doctor. By the end of the first week she had discontinued all her tranquilizing medications, contenting herself with an analgesic which sufficed to keep the headaches within tolerable limits. A therapeutic alliance was beginning to emerge.

The team met for the second time at the end of a two-week period. The task now was to crystallize the plans that had been forming in the minds of the patient, her husband, and the team members as the work had been going on. Team members agreed that this woman was struggling with a concealed psychotic disturbance whose dynamics were reflected in the acceleration of her thought processes, in her disorganized thinking, her poor ego boundaries, and her experiences of depersonalization. Despite the nature of the illness, its chronicity, and her characteristic defensive efforts of manic denial, projection, and somatization, she had shown important assets that included high intelligence, a capacity to reflect psychologically and to be objective about herself and others. The basic strength of her relationship with her husband would stand her in good stead. The patient and her husband were ready to accept a recommendation for individual supportive psychotherapy for the wife, with periodic participation of the husband designed to help the two of them improve their capacity to talk with each other and to explore ways of having a more gratifying sexual relationship. Triavil, an antidepressant, antipsychotic medication, was prescribed, along with a mild analgesic. She was encouraged to refrain from taking other medication except as prescribed by the therapist to whom she would be referred. In a final meeting with the psychiatrist, the social worker, and her husband, the patient was advised to obtain a part-time job and stick to it even if she went through periods of depression and headaches, and to expand her life by participating in church activities and community volunteer work. The letter we received from her a few weeks after she returned home indicates how promptly and fully this woman translated all of these suggestions into action.

This patient is unique, but the method is typical: Team diagnostic work of this sort is one of a variety of diagnostic processes in use at the Menninger Foundation. The decision whether to resort to a formal one- or two-week study, or to do a more conventional consultation, in which the psychiatrist requests various additional studies in the course of the examination as the need arises, is a complicated one. We try to thread our way between the twin dangers of overdiagnosis and underdiagnosis, involving no more people and procedures than necessary—and no less. When a problem is clearly a complex one, and when the ultimate treatment decision may be as weighty as referral for extensive hospital treatment or psychoanalysis, we are likely to plan an extensive study from the beginning. For people who are unsure about whether they need help, or whose financial resources are limited, or who can be seen from preliminary data to be in need of crisis intervention, family therapy, or brief psychotherapy, we begin with a consultation designed either to explore the person's motivation, or to help with the best referral he can afford, or to serve as a beginning for brief psychotherapy.

The kind of study done with Mrs. F. and her husband has special advantages when the problem is severe and chronic and is producing a disruption of family life. Spending a week or two away from home in an unfamiliar setting often facilitates the renunciation of long-standing symptoms such as drug dependency or pathological marital interactions, since the symptomatic behavior is now detached from a thousand daily habit patterns with which the symptoms had become entangled. This brief respite from familiar pain and failure often is a first indication to a person that he can indeed help himself rather than remain a victim or an inflicter of chronic suffering. The emphasis on the patient helping himself is important because the time-limited work with the team minimizes dependent transference reactions both by diffusing these among the members of the team and by keeping in focus from the beginning the fact that an indefinite dependence upon the psychiatrist is not a possibility. At the end of the study, attachments are severed, goodbyes are said (often sad ones on both sides), and a new phase begins.

The work of a psychiatrist is often lonely, and periodic involvement in such a piece of team work—especially when successful—infuses new energy into a depleted clinician's system. Last but not least, the different team members also learn from one another.

The Team Social Worker

Patients who present themselves at the Menninger Foundation for a diagnostic study in most instances are accompanied by family members who are concerned about the patient and his problems. Since the stability of family life depends on the delicate emotional balance and gratifying interaction of its members, the upsetting behavior of one member often makes it difficult, if not impossible, for the family to contain the problems or to find solutions to them. Therefore, it becomes important to study the family as well as the patient during the diagnostic process.

There are two basic reasons for involving the family at the beginning of the diagnostic process:

1. Family members contribute a great deal of essential information which can enhance our understanding of the patient and help us pinpoint the relationship between the individual's problems and the family's problems.

2. In turn, an effective diagnostic process enriches the family's understanding of the problem and makes it more possible for the family to work together in finding appropriate solutions.

In working with families, our overall goals are:

1. To obtain a detailed history of the family and of the presenting symptomatology as the family experiences it;

2. To assess the marital and family dynamics, noting strengths in relationships as well as pathological interactions;

3. To clarify the reality factors which influence what the family can or cannot do to help the patient;

4. To determine the reasons and the extent to which the family should be involved in further treatment; and

5. To convey to the family as well as to the patient our diagnostic impressions and recommendations.

To accomplish these objectives, we begin the diagnostic process with an initial interview in which the psychiatrist and social worker meet with the patient and the family to discuss the presenting problems and to clarify expectations of the examination. Afterward, individual interviews are scheduled to obtain pertinent history and to allow the individual members ample time to discuss their concerns. Additional joint interviews can be helpful and are often necessary to assess the nature of the family interaction and to test ways of modifying communication and/or relationship patterns. At the end of the diagnostic process, the psychiatrist and social worker again meet with the patient and the family to convey impressions and recommendations and to discuss issues which need further clarification.

In the case of Mrs. F., it was clear from the preadmission material that there had been an abrupt change in the marital relationship and thus a marital assessment was indicated. Her husband, who had been a heavy drinker for twenty years, gave up his drinking when she threatened him with divorce. Not only did he successfully give up his drinking, but his behavior reflected his wish to make changes conducive to a more gratifying marriage. While on the surface Mrs. F. seemed to welcome such a change, in reality it caused her to become painfully aware of her loneliness and her inability to have a close relationship with anyone.

Her family history gave us further understanding of her other conflictual relationships. An only child, she had lost her father by divorce and desertion and her mother because of mental illness and institutionalization. She had been unable to have children through miscarriages and had lost her first husband through divorce. She thought she had lost her second husband when his business demands and his drinking problem isolated him from her. However, when she challenged this loss by threatening divorce, she discovered instead a concerned husband who was willing to make personal changes in an effort to preserve and rebuild the marital relationship. In the context of this relationship change, Mrs. F. became aware of her emotional limitations and sought a different kind of personal evaluation for herself and her husband. At the same time her husband began to reflect on his increasing dissatisfaction with the marriage. He realized that both his drinking problem and his wife's constant headaches were largely responsible for their gradually deteriorating social and sexual activities. Although he was not particularly psychologically minded, he was eager to talk about concrete problems, especially sexual difficulties. During the interviews, no attempt was made to uncover with him the historical origin of the sexual problems, but he was receptive to what we might call "bibliotherapy": At the suggestion of the social worker he read and discussed several pertinent books which helped him clarify further some of his own concerns and to share these with his wife.

Diagnostically, the chronicity of Mrs. F.'s symptoms, her traumatic early history, and years of pathological marital interaction indicated a fairly severe emotional problem. On the other hand, her numerous achievements, her receptivity to change, and the growing evidence of an increasing healthier bond with her husband pointed to a more favorable prognosis. Through our detailed discussion at the first team meeting, it became clear that the couple showed potential for a closer and more mutually gratifying relationship which could foster growth in the marriage and help make continued psychological treatment more fruitful.

As this case illustrates, one of the primary goals of the team members is to understand the nature of intrapsychic conflict. A special task of the social worker is to assess the interplay between intrapsychic conflict and family conflict. In this regard, effective communication among team members is crucial. Once the significant data are gathered, there should be either enough internal consistency or enough contradictions among various reports to plan further diagnostic strategy. Often, joint interviews with the patient and various family members become useful to test out initial diagnostic leads and to clarify further the most appropriate treatment intervention for the patient and the family.

The Team Psychologist

When a psychologist does psychological testing, he often does it at the request of another professional, frequently a psychiatrist, in order to answer some question that the referring clinician has about a patient. The psychologist may have little information about the patient other than the diagnostic question at hand, and may have no personal contact with his referral source. The psychologist may then see the patient and carry out testing which enables him to answer the referral question, as he understands it, and to his own satisfaction. A written report—with thanks for the referral if done on a private practice basis, or with a brief conversation or meeting if part of an institutional arrangement—may be the only communication from the psychologist, the psychiatrist then using what he has obtained in the way of new or confirmatory knowledge in his diagnostic or treatment role with the patient.

Some elements of this model are similar to the requests a physician makes for X rays or laboratory studies. Some elements are like that of an internist asking for a consultation by a surgeon, or a speech pathologist getting an opinion from an audiologist. Working in teams, that is, bringing the benefit of multiple perspectives to bear in diagnostic and treatment efforts, can take many forms. Ideally, however, the members of a team should have some particular expertise in the work being carried out, and the structural arrangements should allow each member to make his optimal contribution.

What working arrangements or structures enable a psychologist to contribute optimally when his role is to administer psychological tests? As an integral part of a diagnostic team, a psychologist can first bring his expertise to bear in the formulation of diagnostic questions to be answered. The psychologist's expertise does not reside within the tests themselves, but in the sensitivity and knowledge he acquires through training and experience, and he can assess what contribution testing can likely make to the problem at hand. In some cases, testing may be judged unnecessary when the data available through other sources are sufficient to meet the clinical needs. Ideally, the kind and amount of testing performed should be tailored to the presenting situation, though sometimes a test report is useful later for other purposes. For example, testing originally geared toward assessing a patient's suitability for an expressive psychotherapy might later be used by the therapist to anticipate likely transference paradigms, regressive potential around certain conflict areas, impulse-defense configurations, and so on. Another special point arises when the testing is relied on by colleagues who need support for their observations for reasons of inexperience, lack of confidence, or some form of legal necessity.

Decisions about how the testing should be focused may also grow out of the early test impressions of the psychologist or observations by others on the team. In the case of Mrs. F., the presenting situation dictated a full test battery, since she had never had a comprehensive study and the questions raised at the outset were varied and complex: How can we understand the patient's chronic symptoms on a psychological basis—can we rule out organic factors? In what sort of characterological context does her symptom exist? Are there significant masochistic leanings? Is she a help-rejecting complainer? Does the high degree of organization and clarity in her initial communication with us reflect strength that could be mobilized in the service of change, or hyperalertness in the service of controlling others which could be difficult to work with? With this history of chronic symptoms, will we find resources for responding to psychotherapy? Is more serious disturbance being held tenuously in abeyance?

At the time of the midweek team meeting, two testing sessions had been conducted and it was clear that the patient was struggling mightily to control serious thought disturbance. Her rather bland and detached manner stood in marked contrast to serious inner turmoil, with depression and anxiety accompanying a sense of helplessness, pessimism, and guilt. Alerting the team to the patient's real though not apparent distress, and the potential she had for disorganization and perhaps even suicide, led to changes in the psychiatrist's approach to the patient. This possibility of communication with other team members while an evaluation is in progress is another valuable element of good teamwork. With this patient, testing done and reported following the psychiatric interviews would not have been as useful; testing directed toward circumscribed questions (Is there organic damage? What is the patient's suicide potential?) might not have elicited other important findings: significant intellectual strengths which she could bring to bear on tasks in spite of some encroachment by thought disturbance, and an ability to improve her performance with time and encouragement. These findings suggested a better prognosis than had earlier been judged possible, and proved to be correct, at least from what follow-up we have available.

The Team Consultant

The efficacy of teamwork is further enhanced by an additional member—the team consultant—whose function is crucial in facilitating smooth teamwork. The consultant helps team members recognize their interdependence, the limitations of their partial views, and the need to synthesize these views for the sake of understanding the patient better. Clinical team members must share with their colleagues their knowledge, ignorance, confusion, or frustrations if they are to discover solutions to clinical problems. Such self-exposure is not to be frowned upon as denoting incompetency or insecurity, but should be seen as a mark of professional honesty and maturity.

In our setting, the consultant to a team never sees the patient except indirectly through the eyes of the team members. In this way he maintains a higher degree of objectivity, since he is not subjected to the patient's direct impact on him or prejudiced with preconceived, favorite clinical impressions that are likely to develop were he to interview the patient himself. He remains equidistant from the various team members as the diagnostic mosaic emerges, at first shapelessly, with different pieces of information and different levels of inferences closely juxtaposed.

Because of the position he occupies vis-à-vis the team members, and because of his being invested with a great deal of authority by the members who also hold high expectations of his performance, he is cast in the position of a leader. As one might expect, such a situation is likely to stir up infantile emotions, jealousies, and rivalries among the participants, each wanting to have the greater share of the leader's admiration and attention, or striving to compete with him for supremacy. However, if properly channeled and put to work for the patient's benefit, these dynamics can produce a more accurate and deeper understanding of the patient.

Since the type of examination we are describing fosters the rapid development of intense relationships through daily contact with the patient and his family, it is not surprising that irrational attitudes might propel the team to wish for premature closure, avoidance of painful areas, or rejection of conflicting views in the complicated group process that develops from the team members' interactions. The team consultant is in a position to understand and disentangle such interactions when they become an impediment to the diagnostic objective.

In the case of Mrs. F., when the team met for the first time a week before her arrival, anticipations were mixed. On the one hand, the clarity of the patient's initial request was perceived by some as being "controlling" since obviously she knew what she wanted and was determined to get it. The severity and chronicity of her symptoms made the team feel unenthusiastic about the diagnostic task; they anticipated an unrewarding patient who unconsciously would try to prove the team members impotent as helpers. Her psychopathology was well grasped, as was the fragility of her ego. However, her assets were not perceived with equal clarity, nor spelled out with much conviction. So, with that sense of skepticism, the team began its work. The consultant from the beginning, as he continued to do throughout all the meetings, had to define and redefine the primary task to which the group should address itself: a comprehensive understanding of the patient which could lead to solid recommendations for her improvement and predictions about her response. Indeed, the more a consultant helps the group to see its task clearly and stick to it, the less danger there is of the team being ruled and disrupted by unconscious basic assumptions. As tensions increase and surpass the optimal level necessary for a productive and useful working relationship, the effectiveness of the teamwork might be threatened seriously. Then the consultant must sustain the team members and deal with the anxiety engendered by the frustrations they experience.

In the case of Mrs. F., when the team convened after two days of work, the data available did not appear to gel. The psychiatrist felt she had little impact on Mrs. F. since the patient continued to be testy and suspicious of the psychiatrist's professional credentials. The patient resisted the psychiatrist's efforts to diminish the large amount of medication she was taking. The social worker reported that the husband was a psychologically unsophisticated man, though he appeared interested in the patient's welfare and seemed willing to make sacrifices for her. The psychologist pointed out the patient's easily triggered delusional potential, the evident thought disorder, and the rigidity of her defenses. The psychological tests provided more evidence than was available to any other team member of the patient's capacity to stick to a task, to respond well to structure, and to use her intellectual functions without disturbance from her anxiety. The picture of a woman who had the capacity to think clearly, to organize her thoughts properly, and to communicate informatively was a contrast to the earlier image of a "very sick" patient. The consultant, focusing on the apparent lack of continuity between these two impressions, helped bring together the material that had first appeared to fit poorly, and helped integrate the different inferences drawn from discrepant observations.

It became apparent that the resoluteness of this woman, if properly channeled, could become a definite asset in successfully implementing some treatment recommendations. What previously seemed to be a controlling stance now appeared to be the way she protected herself from inner disorganization that threatened her when situations were not clearly spelled out and her anxiety rose to unmanageable levels.

The psychiatrist, who had been nondirective in her initial contact, remaining rather neutral and inviting the patient to reflect in an open-ended style, now began to question the usefulness of this technique. It became clear that a more supportive and structured type of interview, capitalizing on the patient's assets and making them explicit to her, would be more useful. If this change in approach was in the right direction, then the patient's subsequent attitude and behavior should confirm it, just as an interpretation in a psychotherapeutic hour is confirmed or invalidated by the subsequent material that emerges. When the patient's behavior is kept in the center of all diagnostic discussions, then the danger of formulating interesting but speculative or irrelevant hypotheses is minimized.

We should remember that up to this point the psychiatrist had not been able to persuade Mrs. F. to reduce her medication. It was still an open question as to how much of the behavior we had examined was clouded by the effects of Mrs. F.'s mixture of medications. Her willingness to reduce the use of drugs would become the gauge for measuring her needs to exert control and appear self-sufficient as opposed to her capacity for cooperation and self-reflection. When the psychiatrist changed her interviewing approach, the patient first agreed to diminish her medication and then she discontinued it almost entirely. She became more spontaneous and was able to develop a genuine therapeutic alliance with the psychiatrist.

It was the consultant's task to point out to the team members that all of the feelings they had initially experienced—the hopelessness, unclarity, and frustration about not having a definite direction— reflected Mrs. F.'s own views about her own life. Frequently the same polarizations that the patient experiences in relating to his internal objects are reflected in the reactions of the team members who find themselves unconsciously allied with one aspect or another of the patient's conflicts. Strong group countertransferences can emerge early in the contact with any patient and, if the team understands these factors, they can work with them to gain a different understanding of the patient's functioning and thus attain a conviction about the value and effectiveness of the team itself.

A diagnostic assessment, as conducted by this team, is a complete process with a beginning, a middle, and an end phase. The team consultant has to provide the monitoring function that relates the work of the diagnostic team to the different phases of the process. The end phase is of particular importance, for in that period the team's recommendations are discussed with the patient. Note that they are discussed, not given to a passive recipient. The patient, who has been active in the diagnostic process from the beginning, continues to be an active participant as the end approaches, suggesting and evaluating the treatment alternatives. As timekeeper of the process, the consultant reminds the team of the importance of making time available for working through the treatment recommendations.

Summary

Working in teams, that is, bringing the work of various disciplines together—testing, interviews, social casework, as well as whatever physical studies may be indicated—provides a more accurate and complete picture of the patient than any one of them alone. None of them is the criterion by which the others are measured; none has an inside track on the truth. Mutual respect for the skill of individual team members and for the validity and importance of each point of view is a prerequisite for good teamwork. Integrating data which are virtually identical from these various disciplines is sometimes hard in itself, but to assimilate and organize information from interviews, tests, history, accounts by relatives, school and work records, etc., requires a high degree of conceptual and integrative skill. Apparent contradictions must be reconciled, views must be fit together like pieces of a puzzle, and understanding of a unique individual must emerge. For such teamwork, good communication is essential. If team members are unable to find a common language, the team which could be a tower of strength may become a Tower of Babel. To accomplish their goal of optimal service to patients, team members must be convinced about the worth of their own contribution, trust and rely on the special skills of others on the team, and work toward effective communication.

The kind of diagnostic work we have described is sophisticated, intense, demanding, and expensive. But as this presentation makes clear, for Mrs. F., who had been branded for many years with the label of chronic psychosis, it was a careful diagnosis that made the difference.

DIAGNOSIS IN FAMILY TREATMENT

ARTHUR MANDELBAUM, M.S.W.*

Without diagnostic understanding, the family therapist swims in a sea of chaos. He is pounded by tides of data, fear, anger, apathy, indifference, and sadness; the family dares him to guess their secrets and challenges him to enter their system of operations, codes, and habits they have long practiced to repel outsiders who dare to intrude. From the first moment of contact with a family, the therapist begins the complex process of diagnosis with an ever changing working hypothesis. Although each family member is the concern of the family therapist, he especially focuses on diagnosing the family system—the unique rules of family conduct, the overt and hidden laws governing transactions, the family's interactions in the therapist's presence, and the therapist's own interactions with the family.

Usually a family has already selected one or two members as identified patients whom the therapist is expected to change. Not only are these identified patients troubled and in pain, having symptoms that are causing the family to suffer, but they are also expressing most dramatically for the family its failure to work well as a unit, as an interdependent group of individuals. Family members are either too enmeshed and involved with each other or too distant and fragmented. A knowledge of growth and developmental patterns, of individual and group behavior, and of individual and group

---

* Director, Family Therapy Staff Training Program, The Menninger Foundation, Topeka, Kansas.

pathology must guide the therapist in understanding the special attention the identified patient may require and in understanding how
his symptoms may be expressed as depression, severe and destructive acting out, asthma, anorexia, or other psychosomatic disturbances.

If the therapist determines that the whole family will be the
best medium to effect change, he tests his hypothesis by assisting
the family gradually to shift their emphasis away from the identified
patient toward an examination of their mutual problems in living
together in their various roles as mother, father, spouse, child, sibling, grandparent, cousin, ex-husband, ex-wife, etc., as well as in
dealing with the ghosts who refuse to be buried and the family
secrets that fester. As the family therapist seeks to help the family
accomplish this task, he is evaluating on several levels the flexibility of the family structure—the ways it shapes and reshapes
itself, its capacity for change, its power structure, its alliances, its
subsystems, its sensitivities, and its capacity for giving support to
its members. Within this range of diagnostic data, he must also
be acutely sensitive to and observant of his own impact on the
family as he joins them, accommodates them, opposes them, and
as they absorb him, resist him, swallow him, spit him out, join
against him, resist his interventions, or as they slowly find other,
more creative transactional patterns. Diagnosis blends with the
process and the process blends with diagnosis; they are inseparable.
All acquisition of knowledge and change for the therapist and the
family can be described as the constant revision of hypotheses.

In troubled families, credibility and trust have been impaired
with a consequent loss of real tension and real communication.
An individual receives the most intimate and revealing view of
himself reflected in the eyes of his family members. His special
perspective of himself, his self-concept, his self-esteem, and his
role in the family comes from his position, the particular space
he occupies, within the matrix of his family. When the identified patient feels he can do nothing to improve the quality of family
life or improve his position in the family or rescue his floundering
parents, then he experiences helplessness. He might express this
helplessness by failing to learn, hyperactivity, temper tantrums,
soiling, enuresis, or a variety of psychosomatic symptoms. He

usually will illustrate this helplessness in the initial family interviews by restless, random behavior, withdrawal, unusual physical distance from others, or exhibitionistically demanding to be the center of attention. When the therapist deals actively with the first diagnostic clues of family dysfunction, he begins to acclimatize the family to the real communication and real tension that gradually and eventually build more credibility and trust.

Case example: Each member of the family agreed that Roberta, age twelve, was the baby in the family. Her sister, who was several years older, not only chose Roberta's clothes for her but dressed and fed her as well since she was "incompetent" to do these tasks herself. Roberta, who talked with a pronounced lisp, agreed with this evaluation; she liked the attention. Despite her superior intelligence and attractive appearance, playing the role of infant was the only way she could get close to her mother. She was not aware of this fact and insisted that being at the periphery of the family suited her best. However, at night, when her parents were out, she had nightmares and would not be able to sleep until her mother returned home. When her mother came into the bedroom to check on her, Roberta pretended to be asleep. Although all members of the family agreed she was *their* infant, they considered her persistent questions and demands to be heard as rude, distracting, and intrusive. Roberta then began to develop severe stomach pains which upon comprehensive medical examination had no physical basis. But she had frightened all of them, and the family *now* paid attention to her and hovered around her when she complained of feeling ill.

When the therapist observed this pattern, he gently refused to allow the older sister to speak for Roberta, and he insisted that all must listen when Roberta wanted to speak. When Roberta was silly and offered "foolish" comments, he made the observation that the eye contact between the identified patient and her sister was a curious way to get mothering, since it negated the real mother in the family. He then physically moved Roberta close to the mother. When the family members called Roberta the baby, he pointed out the *fact* that she was the youngest child but at twelve could hardly be considered a baby. Soon Roberta rebuked the family members who called her the baby and resisted her sister's teasing, jealous eye contact. After several sessions, Roberta lost her lisp and was dressing herself, and her physical complaints ceased. However, by this time, the therapist had created in the family a sense of hope that they could now deal with other, more pervasive, more profound family problems.

With a technique called family sculpting, where each family member structures a tableau of the closeness and distance he experiences in relation to each family member as well as the closeness, distance, and characteristic emotional posture of the family members as they interact, the therapist and the family simultaneously obtain a vivid and often startling moving picture (à la Rashomon) of their ritualistic movements. These movements reflect their external and internal views of each other, their views of family life, and may give glimpses of the symbolic meanings of the symptoms presented by the identified patient.

Case example: A wife was angry with her husband because of his "dishonest business practices." She accused him of keeping secrets from her; he accused her of being rigidly puritanical, inquisitive, controlling, and distrustful without cause. As this battle raged, their seventeen-year-old son "sneaked" food from the refrigerator and stored it in his room. Soon there was an epidemic of stealing in the home with every member of the family angry and suspicious of each other. In several sculpting sessions, the children illustrated how money and other valuable possessions were strewn around the house, openly inviting family members to violate each other's territory so they could catch one another in the act of stealing. The children made it quite clear that they were reflecting and reenacting the serious conflicts that raged between the parents.

The direct observation and study of family transactions in which the family members "show and tell" of their lives together give the therapist moving, intensive, and telling glimpses into the spontaneous relationship patterns—the coalitions formed, the power politics, the trading off among members, the family's affective life, the use of content and metaphor to conceal or highlight symbolic struggles. Above all, the therapist looks for those parts of family functioning that work well versus those that work poorly as well as how the family reacts to developmental stress (e.g., death, loss, change of job, physical illness, etc.) and the duration of the conflict and its roots in the past that are still alive and affecting the present. Diagnosis is most accurate when it is based on observations not of the strange and esoteric happenings in family transactions, but of the common practices of family life, those habits and ordinary customs that form the strongest realities and memories for all of us. In one family interview it was something as mundane but extraordinarily significant as the awkward way the father held his six-month-old daughter and his difficulty in helping his overwhelmed wife struggle with a rebellious three-year-old. When these observations were pointed out to him, he expressed his anger and sadness because he had opposed his wife's wishes to have children and did not feel he was a capable father. The therapist must rely on ". . .the exploration and clarification of the nature and sources of family difficulties as a means of resolving these difficulties. The immediate, on-going transactions of family members with one another and with the therapists are regarded as the most significant starting-point data to be explored and understood" (Wynne 1965, p. 290).

In family therapy, the diagnosis emerges out of a new frame of reference. In this new context, the major scrutiny is on the direct observation of the here and now transactions between family members, a penetrating look at the emotional system of family life. Framo (1972) suggests that psychopathology, which is usually seen as an insoluble, intrapsychic conflict, may now be seen as ". . . a special form of relationship event which occurs between intimately related people" (p. 271). He postulates ". . . that symptoms are formed, selected, faked, exchanged, maintained, and reduced as a function of the relationship context in which they are naturally embedded" (p. 273).

There is no better way to observe the phenomenon of irrational role assignments or projective transference distortions than to observe a family unit as it functions in a treatment situation. Nor is there any better way to observe the phenomenon of symptoms developing and reproducing themselves than to watch the family as it deepens its transactions in a treatment session. Here the therapist can evaluate the varying levels of emotional strength in family members, the psychological sensitivities in each, their intellectual endowment, physical and psychological stamina, communication patterns, flexibilities, power exchanges, emotional chain reactions, repetitive and predictable patterns, functional states which enhance development, and dysfunctional patterns which retard growth. Each person in the family is labeled and given a role that is as powerful a determinant of behavior as genetic endowment.

As the therapist acquires knowledge of the family and its own particular and unique structure, he will be buffeted by many currents, especially by an inner turmoil that reflects his experience of the family's impact on him—perhaps pulling him into their fears, bewilderments, and confusions, or excluding him. Sometimes all these contradictory forces occur simultaneously. These engulfing influences upon the therapist are an invaluable component in the diagnostic process and will shape the nature and power of the interventions to follow. The therapist may enter directly into the family's interactions in order to break the futile pathways of communication, to alter repetitive stresses, and to assist the family experience the effect of his shifts and his refusal to be drawn into their chaos.

The therapist may employ other techniques to turn the family's attention toward using their own powers of observation concerning their struggles. By using the sculpting technique, he may lead the family into actions that reveal ". . . aspects of the family's inner life that have remained hidden. Vague impressions and confused feelings on the periphery of awareness are given form through physical and spatial expression" (Papp et al. 1973, p. 202). Or the therapist may use the mapping and structural techniques developed by Minuchin (1974) or the paradoxical framework presented by Haley (1973) and Watzlawick et al. (1974). In describing the latter technique, Watzlawick et al. (1974) place less importance on etiology than on the initial struggle to define the current problem in the clearest, most concrete terms. As a second step they advise a brief exploration of those past and current efforts to solve the family problem—efforts that have only succeeded in sinking the family more deeply into the quagmire it has created for itself. The more change attempted under such circumstances, the more the system remains the same. Quoting Wittgenstein that ". . . 'for an answer which cannot be expressed the question too cannot be expressed' " (pp. 112–13), Watzlawick *et al.* believe the third step is a clear definition of what concrete changes can be achieved. Their fourth suggestion is that the therapist formulate and implement a plan to produce change—a plan based on confronting the family with the unexpected, the paradox, to produce change directed toward realistic and appropriate goals rather than utopian aims.

Bowen's (1965) approach to diagnosis is to shift the frame of reference sharply away from individual pathology toward both family pathology and the relationship system that has developed over many generations. Every day family members are enmeshed within ambivalent relationships which are deeply influenced by their ancestral lives and which they are compelled to repeat. Bowen's concept is that the family, with its emotional fusion and undifferentiated ego mass, is the unit of illness. The core dynamic structure is a triangle—two people involve a third in a futile attempt to solve their problems. Bowen describes the dysfunctioning family as a collection of individuals fighting to maintain their solidarity against change as well as struggling for their individuation and autonomy. Possessed by each family member, this eternal conflict, the struggle to be part of the family as well as to be different, is one that could lead to emotional sterility or to appropriate independence and vigor.

The diagnostician in family therapy presses toward the center of a historical problem while, paradoxically, creating a setting in which family members can enact the current structure that inhibits their growth. Paradoxically, too, family members not only press him to understand and solve their problems which increases the pressure on the therapist to enter the conflict, but they also try to drive and keep the therapist away from understanding the mysteries of their family structure. This conflicting, contrasting pressure makes it difficult for the therapist to maintain diagnostic clarity. When the therapist begins to understand which doors to open first, then the family can dare to hope for change and to consider new and less frightening ways to risk it.

References

BOWEN, MURRAY: Family Psychotherapy with Schizophrenia in the Hospital and in Private Practice. In *Intensive Family Therapy: Theoretical and Prac-*

tical Aspects, Ivan Boszormenyi-Nagy & J. L. Framo, eds., pp. 213–43. New York: Harper & Row, 1965.

FRAMO, J. L.: Symptoms from a Family Transactional Viewpoint. In *Progress in Group and Family Therapy*, C. J. Sager & H. S. Kaplan, eds., pp. 271–308. New York: Brunner/Mazel, 1972.

HALEY, JAY: *Uncommon Therapy: The Psychiatric Techniques of Milton H. Erickson*. New York: Norton, 1973.

MINUCHIN, SALVADOR: *Families and Family Therapy*. Cambridge, MA: Harvard University Press, 1974.

PAPP, PEGGY et al.: Family Sculpting in Preventive Work with "Well Families." *Fam. Process* 12(2):197–212, 1973.

WATZLAWICK, PAUL et al.: *Change: Principles of Problem Formation and Problem Resolution*. New York: Norton, 1974.

WYNNE, L. C.: Some Indications and Contraindications for Exploratory Family Therapy. In *Intensive Family Therapy: Theoretical and Practical Aspects*, Ivan Boszormenyi-Nagy & J. L. Framo, eds., pp. 289–322. New York: Harper & Row, 1965.

INDICATIONS AND CONTRAINDICATIONS FOR GROUP PSYCHOTHERAPY

LEONARD HORWITZ, Ph.D.*

A large percentage of patients who are capable of profiting from a dyadic approach can benefit equally well from group treatment. But it is also true that some patients should be excluded from groups, while for others group psychotherapy is the treatment of choice. For the most part diagnostic categories are relatively useless in helping us with the problem of selection. Rather, certain important personality dimensions and aspects of functioning play a major role. The following comments are not intended to be an exhaustive discussion of this topic, but rather will introduce some of the main considerations relative to the problem of selection.

Perhaps the most general consideration relates to the issue of the patient's capacity to stick with treatment. The diagnostician must constantly ask himself, "Is this person capable of withstanding the frustrations of a group experience, especially in the early phases, and remain with the group for a sufficiently long period of time?" The achievement of stable personality change, whether in group or in individual treatment, usually requires a lengthy period of therapeutic work. Dropouts tend to be greater in group than in individual treatment because frustrations tend to outweigh gratifications to a greater extent in a group situation, especially in the early phases. Thus, it becomes doubly important to utilize careful

* Director, Group Psychotherapy Service, The Menninger Foundation, Topeka, Kansas.

selection procedures and to prepare the patient thoroughly before he is accepted into the group.

Let us deal first with the problem of contraindications. One major contraindication to a group referral is the presence of an acute crisis situation. Whether the crisis is mainly situational, such as a recent loss of a significant figure, or is associated with an acute personality decompensation, a group is not an ideal setting for managing such problems. The patient who is undergoing such critical difficulties needs active, supportive interventions best obtained in a one-to-one relationship. Furthermore, a patient in crisis is an inordinate drain on the group's time. However, once a patient is already in a group and such a situation arises, the problem should be handled in the group, although additional parameters may be introduced during a period of great stress.

A second contraindication to group referral is a marked depression or a strong suicidal potential. Psychomotor retardation and difficulty in talking make it unwise to attempt to treat a marked dysphoria with group techniques. Similarly, there are too many possibilities for evasion and concealment in a group setting which would work to the detriment of the suicidal patient.

A third contraindication is the existence of a low tolerance for anxiety and frustration. A group often tends to induce frustration due to competition among members for its time and attention. A common wish is to become the favorite "child." Although support is also an important dimension of the group experience, it may be overshadowed by anxiety in the opening phases of group membership. Patients who deal with heightened tension by engaging in destructive or self-destructive actions, who tend to take flight in reaction to anxiety, are best excluded from a group.

Finally, people with strong paranoid propensities find the group extremely painful and difficult to use therapeutically. The heightened stimulation of several participants tends to exacerbate the patient's paranoid fears and makes him even more distrustful than he would be in a private interview with a professional who understands the patient's special needs and fears.

With regard to positive indications, the group situation highlights narcissistic problems, bringing out in bold relief a patient's egocentrism, abrasiveness, and greed. A patient in group therapy must be able to share the time of the group with others. Also, an inability to take an interest in others, to delay gratification of one's own needs while attempting to help another, are character defects that are flagrantly exhibited by infantile patients. These problems emerge with clarity and speed in a group setting and provide the therapist with special therapeutic leverage, if the patient can tolerate the anxiety and frustration of the process.

Group psychotherapy also may be the treatment of choice for those individuals who experience extreme degrees of shyness, timidity, and inhibition in a social setting. The sources for such social neuroses are as varied as their manifestations, although leading dynamic factors consist of low self-esteem, a fear of uncontrolled aggression, and a reaction formation to exhibitionistic strivings. Frequently such people account for their social withdrawal and silence in the group by asserting they lack the wisdom to help others. But, with encouragement, they usually learn that they are indeed more capable than they had believed and that their contributions are valued and appreciated. Furthermore, the fear of one's aggressive impulses often will diminish as the individual witnesses aggressive interactions which do not damage a relationship. A frequent comment made by successfully treated patients is that they experience a much greater comfort in their social interactions with others, particularly in social groups.

Finally, adolescence and young adulthood typically bring up the kinds of conflicts which lend themselves to effective work in groups. Erikson* has described this period as a time of struggle toward the establishment of an identity (as opposed to role diffusion), and the young person in the throes of this identity crisis needs group acceptance and confirmation. He must have his abilities, talents, and personal characteristics valued by society as a whole and by peers in particular. A related developmental task is that of liberating oneself from parental figures, often characterized by adolescent rebellion. At this stage, young people are more receptive to the influence of their peers than to ambivalently held authority figures. Hence their suitability for treatment in a group.

These issues constitute some of the major diagnostic considerations involved in the selection of patients for a group modality.

---

* Erikson, E. H.: *Childhood and Society*, Ed. 2. New York: Norton, 1963.

WHAT THE PSYCHOANALYTIC GROUP PSYCHOTHERAPY SITUATION EVOKES

DONALD COLSON, Ph.D.*

Patients in group psychotherapy often encounter difficulties with at least three aspects of the group: first, the complexity and ambiguity of the situation; second, the relationships among the group members; and third, the relationship of the group members with the psychotherapist. If we understand what the psychoanalytic group psychotherapy situation contains and evokes, we might better determine which people should be referred to this treatment modality.

The Group as a Complex, Ambiguous Social Situation

In comparison with most nontreatment situations, group psychotherapy provides a more complex and ambiguous social situation than people are accustomed to. The ambiguity of the situation is increased by the presence of a number of people, i.e., the patient's fears of what may emerge tend to be greater in the group than in individual therapy. Added to the patient's concerns about what may emerge in himself, he may fear the reactions of others and what such reactions will evoke. When a patient first enters the group, he must contend with his reactions to a novel and stressful situation as well as with the fantasies aroused in other patients about a new member. For some patients, this novel situation is pleasurably

* Staff Psychologist and Senior Investigator in the Group Psychotherapy Follow-Up Research Project, The Menninger Foundation, Topeka, Kansas.

challenging. For others, an increase of uncertainty and conflict and the task of finding an acceptable place for themselves are profoundly disturbing. To them, the group poses a threat of being "swallowed up" and deprived of whatever tenuous sense of identity they have achieved. Such patients will either leave the group prematurely or become frozen in a fixed position which will allow little therapeutic benefit.

For example, a person prone to being overwhelmed by increases in internal pressures will be the first one to speak when group pressures increase. His comments are likely to be rambling and disorganized. His weak, passive ego leaves him vulnerable to acting as a barometer for whatever pressures are generated in the group. Probably he would have the same difficulty managing tension in one-to-one expressive treatment. The therapist might consider the possibility of referring this person to a more structured and supportive psychotherapy.

Interaction Among Group Members

Unlike individual psychotherapy, group therapy confronts patients with the task of interacting with a number of other people. The fact that patients are often talking to one another rather than focusing attention on the therapist allows the therapist freedom to study obstacles to meaningful interaction and to assist patients to understand and overcome such obstacles. For some patients, the opportunity to interact with others creates an atmosphere in which certain assets can develop, for example, leadership, empathy, helping behavior in all forms, and the ability to obtain help from others. For such patients, the group facilitates a sense of cohesion and common purpose. They feel less lonely or isolated and more comforted by the support of the other patients. They learn they are not alone in having problems and that disturbed people can be helpful. For patients who are conspicuously lacking in social skills and feel themselves without social resources, the group may be intolerably stressful. Most therapy groups can accommodate surprisingly wide variations in types of people, but if a patient is too "different" and is unable to find common ground for talking with the others, he may be scapegoated and further excluded. A related issue is that because patients share each other's time and attention, competitive feelings are stirred up which may be intolerable to the patient who feels resourceless or powerless.

The following are examples of difficulties which arise in the relationships of group members:

1. One patient in the group may be emotionally insensitive. He seems ignorant about feelings, with the result that he is tactless, too blunt, and asks naive, "rude" questions. He may unwittingly help the group progress by pioneering a discussion of issues which the other group members are afraid to approach. However, in working with such a patient, it is important for the therapist to determine how to help the group assist the patient to come into better contact with emotion without feeling overwhelmed or without decompensating.

2. A patient with prominent masochistic features irritates the other group members, often becoming scapegoated. He puts himself last in line for the group's attention. He thinks he is not worth the time, that everyone else is more worthy. The therapist looks for information about the rigidity of this pattern of interaction and assesses which interventions might assist the patient to interact with the others on a more equal footing, and thereby enhance his self-esteem.

3. A rather competitive patient who relies heavily on narcissistic defenses is contemptuous of the other group members. He openly states his opinion that there is little benefit to be derived from talking with "patients." He makes an effort to draw people out; but because he reveals little about himself and attempts to control the group, he provokes rejection by the other group members. The therapist can help the group examine this interaction. If the patient can fully recognize his impact on others, he might feel motivated to find more adaptive ways of relating to the other group members.

Interaction Between Group Members and Therapist: Transference

Because patients in a group are not solely dependent on the therapist, they often support one another in particular stances toward the therapist. So the patient may oppose the therapist's interventions in more obvious ways than he would employ in an individual setting. This pattern means that the patient may come to experience various aspects of himself in more dramatic ways. For the patient who can occasionally step back emotionally and take a more objective look at his experience, this exaggeration of the resistance can be a significant part of learning and growth. Similarly, the enhancement of constructive and creative aspects of the patient's behavior may build self-esteem. On the other hand, a patient who for one reason or another is unable to shift perspectives might end up as a permanent spokesman for the group's opposition to psychological work at the expense of his learning.

An additional matter influencing the way transference is manifested in the group relates to the fact that all members share the time and attention of the group therapist. Many patients in group therapy speak of their longing for a dyadic relationship with the therapist. This aspect of the group often enhances feelings of deprivation, competition, and guilt about taking one's fair share, thereby in fantasy depriving other group members of time with the therapist. An important issue for the patient's use of the group is whether he can occasionally take enough distance from his dependent longings and the depriving aspects of the experience to learn something more about himself. He might learn, for example, about possible alternatives to the self-defeating ways in which he responds to his wishes to have something more. Another patient who can neither function autonomously nor tolerate dependent wishes might experience the therapist as malevolent and grossly distort or ignore his comments. Types of problems that commonly arise are:

1. The patient who insatiably demands more from the therapist feels driven by the need for satisfaction and views the therapist as the sole source of supply. Thus, he is oblivious to the therapist and to the other group members as human beings. His personality makes him well suited to be spokesman for the group's view of the therapist as depriving and of themselves as insatiable. There may be serious questions as to whether this patient can derive sufficient support from the group and can tolerate the sense of helpless dependence and frustration long enough to work through such feelings.

2. The person whose major concern is whether the therapist likes him dwells in inordinate detail on what the therapist says in an

eager search for indications of the therapist's feeling for him. This person is concerned with obtaining the love of the therapist, much as a small child who constantly asks his mother, "Mommy, do you like me?" A crucial issue is whether and how the patient can be helped to value his contributions and those of other group members.

3. An individual who falls along the masochistic-paranoid dimension takes for granted that the therapist rejects him. The more dominant the paranoid component, the more certain the patient is that the therapist's comments imply harsh criticism and rejection of him. He may attempt to solicit the help of other group members to devalue the therapist, thereby avoiding a sense of humiliation and rejection. If he is too abrasive and unrelenting in such efforts, he may be ostracized by the group. In any event, the group setting may be too threatening to this patient to allow learning.

In summary, the group therapy patient's major task is to find a place for himself in the group, or a compromise between his personality and needs and those of the group. If he is able to stay and negotiate this challenge, he and the group will gradually discover how he is like the others as opposed to how he is unique. This ongoing process enhances esteem for oneself and others, results in self-understanding, and is one of the most significant vehicles for the therapeutic work. However, some patients are either too disturbed or too "deviant" to derive support from their peers or to make accommodations to others without feeling excessively threatened or devalued. For them, group psychotherapy is not the treatment of choice.

DIAGNOSIS OF ORGANIZATIONS, COMMUNITIES, AND POLITICAL UNITS

TOBIAS BROCHER, M.D.*

The evolution of psychiatric diagnosis has been affected by more than twenty-five years of intensive research in the area of collective influence and group impact on individual behavior. Classic publications (Asch 1940, 1951, 1952; Bion 1948a, 1948b, 1949a, 1949b, 1950a, 1950b, 1952; Cartwright & Zander 1960; Lewin 1951; Lewin et al. 1939; Sherif 1935, 1953) have produced a tendency to question the idealized autonomy of the individual. Freud was accused by his contemporaries of having caused a serious narcissistic injury to individual self-esteem by diagnosing the dependency of the ego as a continuous struggle with two powerful adversaries: the "upward" drive impulses of the id and their "downward" control by the superego as the heir of early aggression. In his first publication on groups, "Group Psychology and the Analysis of the Ego," Freud (1921) stated that group members follow the same ego ideal. Thus, group members reduce ingroup tension and aggression by unifying their individual aggressive drive needs which can then be directed toward an outside object—a particular outgroup or cause. The reduction of infighting and the increase in group cohesion enable the designated leader to use and direct the group's collective power to facilitate the group's success in reaching its goals.

Of course, the individual can become the victim of collective irrational assumptions by being unable to resist the group's pressure.

---

* Director, Center for Applied Behavioral Science, The Menninger Foundation, Topeka, Kansas.

As long as a group is not subject to appropriate control by external reality factors, its members are blinded in their cohesion by the same ego ideal, which is never questioned in terms of reality and group environment. One of the most terrifying collective experiences in recent history was the deliberately planned mass seduction of Germany. Nazi "group think" (Janis 1958) misled millions of people who considered themselves intelligent human beings into a dehumanizing racism that ended in holocaust and cold-blooded slaughter. Sherif and Sherif's (1953) group experiments and Milgram's (1965) punishment research have demonstrated the impact and consequences of irrational premises and group assumptions on individual behavior. It is possible to destroy or divert individual insight and prevent reality perceptions by creating social dependency needs, thereby forcing the individual into primary process operations through collective regression in the interest of collective unconscious drive needs and satisfaction.

Mental health professionals have been confronted with a whole new area of psychiatric diagnosis which can no longer be handled exclusively by separating one individual from the group and treating the isolated patient with traditional methods. The usual argument for limiting diagnosis to single individuals is: Since it is so difficult to determine the intrapsychic dynamics and to understand the motivation and functions of a single person and since the functioning of organizations is determined by so many different persons, how can we dare to try to understand the functioning of organizations, communities, and political units? The dynamics of these interpersonal and intergroup relationships are predetermined by the perception and reaction formations of individuals who form any group, independent of its size. However, the whole is more than the sum of its parts because the various relationships between individuals within the system or organization determine the analytical approach to organizational diagnosis.

In the various approaches used to diagnose organizations, one serious pitfall has been transferring methods appropriate to an individual patient to whole organizations. Applying unchanged psychiatric categories to groups or to society leads to presumptuous diagnostic statements which are based on the assumption that psychiatry and psychology have a valid, objective yardstick for what can be labeled "normal" or "sick." However, such statements do not include the premise that these sciences are part of the same society with their own organizations which do not function any better than the society and which share many basic assumptions with other groups and organizations within the same culture. The obstacle blurring our diagnostic vision is precisely "our acquired psychology —the programmed set of needs, values, attitudes and prejudices . . . which have been shaped and deeply fixed by our existent social institutions" (Marmor 1974, p. 429) and by the organizational mechanisms which we claim to diagnose and change. The question is: How much is the tendency to act to our own advantage or in our own defense connected with the specific needs of the societal group we serve? Psychiatry as an organization will have to redefine its primary task in relation to the environment in terms of reality control.

Organizations created to serve and facilitate human needs "acquire a life of their own, a functional autonomy . . . by virtue of which they thenceforth play a profoundly important role in shaping the personalities of human beings who grow up in their sphere of influence" (Marmor 1974, p. 421) and who begin to serve and maintain it without recognizing the destructive nature of an autonomous organization that neglects human needs. The myth of the machine prevails when the individual submits himself to the autonomy of the institution without questioning the validity of this abstraction. The preliminary diagnostic question, therefore, deals with the relationship between the individual and the organization. It is difficult to give a clear definition of the term *organization* because it is used in such varying contexts. For psychiatric diagnosis, organization must be more narrowly defined than in sociology or anthropology.

In defining the four pure types of complex formal organizations, the distinctions are between variations in costs, benefits, and transactions with recipients. Although most real organizations' actions fulfill the definition of more than one type, they are mixtures and not compounds.

   a. A *cooperative organization* is one whose sponsors are the recipients of its outputs and whose sponsors' goal is their own welfare as recipients. . . . the costs and benefits [are assigned] to them in their role as recipients, not as sponsors, since it is only to receive its outputs that they sponsor the organization . . . .

b. A *profit organization* is one run in the interests of its sponsors, who except incidentally are not the same people as the recipients and whose outputs go to recipients on the basis of selfish transactions.

c. A *service organization* is one whose outputs go to recipients on the basis of generous transactions. In the pure case . . . the outputs are pure gifts whose costs are borne solely by the sponsors.

d. A *pressure organization* is an organization . . . whose outputs go directly or indirectly to [a] recipient . . . for the purpose of improving the position of [the sponsor] . . . in a transactional relation with [the recipient] . . . . The sponsor . . . or his agent bears the cost . . . of the pressure activity . . . which is the output of the organization [Kuhn 1974, p. 323].

Diagnosis is based on organizational analysis which includes two distinct types: ". . . the system concepts to deal with the organization viewed as a unit and the intersystem concepts of communication and transaction to deal with the interactions of its parts and its own interactions as a unit with other systems" (Kuhn 1974, p. 327). The role of the psychiatrist and psychologist is limited to dealing with the intersystem concept. Nevertheless, the psychiatric or psychological consultant must compare his data with the prevailing sociological concept of the total organization as a unit.

However, in spite of the fact that the psychiatrist working as a consultant in business, industry, and government has to cope with the individual organization as a whole, his task is limited to specific aspects. For example, the psychiatrist examines the intra- and intergroup relationships relevant for the functioning of the organization. He looks at an individual's internal processes and at his maintenance system in contrast to the control system. "In all his communications and transactions the individual human acts as a unit—even if with vacillations, contradictions, and unconscious components" (Kuhn 1974, pp. 297–98). By contrast, an organization's external interactions can be carried on simultaneously by different levels of the system. Organizational diagnosis follows these specific patterns by attending separately to the main or whole system level and the subsystem level while dealing also with the intra- and intersystem aspects at each level. In addition, the distinction between formal and informal organizations and between controlled and uncontrolled systems must be made. Since it is possible to gather information about the goals, the internal and external constraints of formal organizations, a detailed theory could be built around formal organizations; however, applying any such theory to informal organizations such as political groups and subgroups would be difficult.

The sociologist has two main choices in the analysis of complex organizations when their complexity becomes too unwieldy to apply a tight analytic mode. He can either use statistical generalizations based on empirical observations of particular types of organizations and their behavior or he can develop a special purpose or simulation model constructed from the same analytic building blocks. The sociological organization theory can still miss relevant aspects important for the diagnostic process because it is less related to organizational structure than to human needs. The diagnostic gap in sociological and economic or structural organization analysis has been the human factor. Gouldner (1965) describes the first steps to correct the sociological model, but his description does not clarify the importance of psychoanalysis as an applied psychology and behavioral science. Gouldner points out the characteristic differences between the social engineering model and the clinical model including psychoanalysis. The traditional management consultant firm often takes the client's own formulation of the client's problems at face value, thereby paradoxically preserving the tensions and neglecting the breakdown in informal organization. In contrast, practitioners employing the clinical model do not accept "their clients' own formulation of their problem . . . at face value. Instead . . . [they take] their clients' complaints and self-formulations as only one among a number of 'symptoms' useful in helping them to arrive at their own diagnosis of the clients' problems" (Gouldner 1965, p. 13). Thus, the social engineer tends to study what the client tells him to, while the clinician necessarily arrives at an independent identification of the group's or organization's problems.

Before discussing more specific details, I should define the general framework within which the psychiatrist can operate to achieve an appropriate organizational diagnosis.

Social scientists who use survey methods in their research on complex organizations do not think of themselves as having much in common with clinicians . . . . [The distinction seems to be apparent in the] quantitative, statistical, content-specific approach . . . [of the social scientist and] the qualitative, nonstatistical, more encompassing approach of the clinician . . . . [Both social scientists and clinicians] are interested in understanding what factors are related to organizational functioning and individual member behavior. . . . [and] in individual and organizational variables, how they relate to one another, and how these relationships change over time [Neff 1965, p. 23].

By the term *diagnosis* the psychiatrist means

. . . the process of examining various characteristics of an organization and its members to provide an accurate description of how things stand or are proceeding . . . . [Diagnosis requires] the collection of valid information . . . evaluation of that information, and assignment of priorities to courses of action which might be taken to improve the state of the organization. A diagnosis . . . is conditioned by the purpose, method, and sophistication of those making it [Neff 1965, p. 25].

Most organizations are

. . . hierarchically structured. This structure can be thought of as a pyramid of 'organizational families.' Each family is composed of a supervisor and the people who report to him, starting with the president and going down through the 'link-pins' (member of one family, head of the next lower) to the first line supervisor and his subordinates [Neff 1965, p. 28].

This structure serves as a communication link upward and a boundary function downward.

The typical member of an average company rarely has full qualitative and quantitative data about the state of the organization's structure. Nevertheless, each subgroup or subsystem within an organization follows certain assumptions that are related to specific reference groups. These reference groups serve as a yardstick of comparison for negative or positive identification. Identifications are motivated by individual aspirations. Hence, the willingness to identify with an organization's overall goals and objectives demonstrates a specific gradient which decreases from the top level down to the production line worker—a factor based on the amount of knowledge and information about the whole. The most striking result of this identification process is the development of an organizational ideology or myth which often shows characteristics of the leading group's values and beliefs. These values are unconsciously shaped by the leader's early object relationships and by historical figures—a sort of "tribal" value. Even the "tribal totem" appears as a trademark, logo, or traditional identifying symbol, just as the unwritten taboos determine inclusion or exclusion from the leading part of the organization.

In the last fifty years most industrial and business organizations have shifted from family enterprise to management systems. For instance, at the beginning of this century one of the largest companies had 1000 employees, but today the average employee does not know the size of the corporation for which he works. In the family enterprise, identification with the founder contributed to the traditional, emotionally rooted feelings of belonging; the exchangeability, anonymity, and the functional concepts of management systems have taken away this emotional potential for personal relationships, creating instead feelings of alienation, isolation, and anxiety that cannot be shared openly with others. Nevertheless, complex organizations are still managed by people. Despite the increase in size and the diversification of production within large corporations, most organizations still consist of clearly distinguishable subsystems which are functionally connected. In addition to the imprinting quality of leadership styles within top management, this connecting function—the "link-pin"—between subsystems is most significant for organizational diagnosis.

In contrast, communities cannot be considered formal organizations. Although the community has a formal leadership and administration, both are only part of the whole, while the population forming the community remains an uncontrolled system. When a team from the Menninger Foundation intervened in the clashes between police and demonstrators in the community of Lawrence, Kansas (Satten *et al.* 1970–71), it became evident that a diagnostic assessment of community conflict must take into account the unstructured and uncontrolled parts of community systems. The informal organization of the unrecognized opinion leaders within the

community who had no official function proved to be more important for gathering diagnostic data than the formal administrative
structure. Similar experiences in other larger communities (Green
et al. 1972) confirm the importance of making the communication
gaps present in intergroup conflicts the primary diagnostic focus.
Although this information cannot be obtained by observation—it
must be provided by individuals—the human factor is often neglected. No intervention is possible without clarifying the interpersonal motivation of intra- and intergroup conflicts.

When dealing with communities or political units like city coun-
cils or school boards as compared with industrial or business organizations, the diagnostic approach employed must take into
account the relevance of highly complex informal and uncontrolled
structures which are difficult to identify. A recent diagnostic study
of a community by another Menninger Foundation team (Brocher
et al. 1975) demonstrates the serious consequences of failing to
identify and involve informal groups and opinion leaders. Not only
is the relevance of informal subgroups often misjudged or unrecognized by traditional, formal community leaders, but their impact
and influence on decision-making processes is frequently underestimated. The residuals of powerful authoritarian leadership assumptions are counterproductive to the intended goals.

When William C. Menninger (1967) studied the leadership styles
of military commanders, he made discoveries similar to Bion's
(1948a, 1948b, 1949a, 1949b, 1950a, 1950b)—that the derivatives of
early object relations in the individual leader determine the preferred, irrational basic assumptions of the group. The more differentiated findings also confirmed the reciprocity between the
individual valences of group or unit members and the specific va-
lence of the group leader. Further development of group theories
led to a more differentiated hypothesis of group functioning. Special
identifiable functions can be recognized within groups and subsystems independent of the technical content or professional task.
We call the role of the formal group leader within an organization
the "alpha function." It is necessarily accompanied by a number
of "alpha variations" taken by leaders of subsystems who are identifying themselves with the primary "alpha." The "alpha function"
could not exist without the majority of followers whose activities

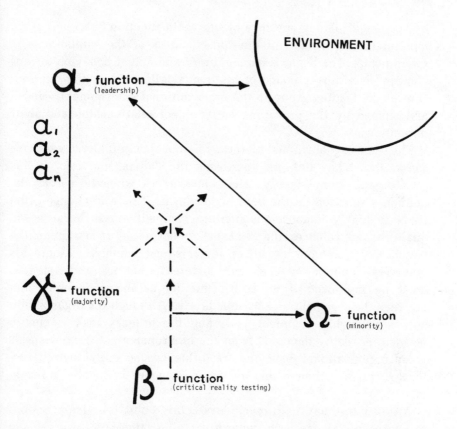

comprise the "gamma function." The relationship of all "gamma functions" to the various "alpha functions" depends on two factors: (1) the relationship between "alpha functions" and "omega functions," i.e., the relation between the leading part and the weakest, most endangered, or temporarily dysfunctional parts of an organization; and (2) the relationship between "alpha functions" and "beta functions," i.e., the specific relation between the leading part and its critical opponent.

The "beta function" represents the independent reality control within a group and introduces the neglected or denied awareness of irrational group assumptions based on emotional group needs without appropriate realistic data. It is usually the most rejected function although the data base stems from realistic observations of how "omega functions" are treated by "alpha" and consequently by "gamma." The importance of the "beta function" becomes more understandable in light of the consequences of the "alpha-omega" relationship. The leader's perception of and actual behavior toward "omega" is a mirror image of his own relationship or the relationship of the leading group to the organizational environment, caused and shaped by the prevailing early object relationships and their derivatives.

The same organizational hierarchy is repeated in the organization's subgroups. The "link-pin" performs the "alpha function" in his own organizational family. His role changes when he serves the boundary function on the next higher level. This role change often leads to highly unconscious ingroup competitiveness because the qualities and valences the "link-pin" must adopt in assuming the "alpha function" on the lower level persist when he adopts his boundary function even though different qualities and valences must be mobilized if he is to function as the connecting link between the organization's various levels. Although the organization may have highly technical goals and the primary task is clearly defined by reality demands from the environment, it is no surprise when organizational decisions are influenced by individual character structures, although this irrational influence is usually unrecognized.

An example may help demonstrate this point. A vice-president in charge of the research department of a large company refused to move to the top executive suite in the main building. In his resistance against a newly appointed executive vice-president, he even refused to participate in various executive committee sessions, pretending that his scientific experiments did not permit him to spend time on administrative issues. As a result the executive committee was confronted with serious personnel problems throughout the research department as well as with an increasing deficit. What appeared on the surface to be an economic problem was actually a character problem in one man who was performing a secondary "alpha function." The struggle continued as long as the organization permitted him to act out and let his character structure take precedence over organizational necessities.

One of the most difficult problems in organizations is the tendency to force individuals into specific roles. Scapegoating in groups is a well-known phenomenon. More specific is the risk of being forced into a certain role that enables other team or group members to avoid burdensome tasks or personal exposure. The same applies to intergroup relations in organizations, as the Ahmedabad, Glacier Company, Unilever, and Findus experiments have proven. The relationship between work assignment, individual capacity, and compensation has been described by Jaques (1961) as the most valid factor for diagnosing and evaluating individual function or dysfunction in an appropriate way as well as diagnosing intergroup prejudice. Most of these research experiences published by the Tavistock Institute of London are based on psychoanalytic concepts. Unfortunately, in some countries psychoanalysis has taken a one-sided direction of dealing mainly with individual psychopathology and technical problems of treatment. We can only regret this loss, although many Europeans have begun to rediscover some of the earlier directions of applied psychoanalysis. The terminology has slightly changed but what is now encompassed by the term *psychosocial factor* was known but abandoned during the 1920s because of unsolved intragroup conflicts within the psychoanalytic organization. However, it has always been part of psychoanalytic theory. It is comforting to recognize that psychoanalysis as an organizational structure can suffer from the same symptoms as other organizations when the human factor is temporarily neglected.

The intraorganizational dynamics of interrelated functions are not abstractions, and none of these functions can be performed by other than human beings. Whatever automated programs may achieve, they cannot work without human beings—human beings who are motivated by psychological needs such as well-being, the search for a stable environment, reduction of fear through predictability, recognition, satisfaction, communication, and trust. Since each individual has to perform organizational functions in the interest of his defined primary tasks, the interrelatedness of these various functions determines the specific problems of organizational diagnosis. The psychiatrist must avoid the trap of accepting the irrational group assumption that one group or one individual is to blame for dysfunctional symptoms. Our recent experience during the worldwide monetary crisis has again confirmed the fact that the individual executive suffers from increasing anxiety and fear because the changing circumstances deprive him of his main virtue, to arrive at rationally based predictions. The symptomatology shows all variations of illnesses, described by Selye (1956) as an accumulation of stress through intrapsychic conflict between ego-ideal and social reality.

The description of interrelated functions within organizational systems and subsystems forms a highly abstract and complex theoretical level of organizational theory. However, before any descriptive phenomenology can become the basis for an organizational theory or philosophy, it must be recognized that organizational functions are predominantly determined by people who continuously negotiate their personal needs for satisfaction and well-being on various levels and under varying conditions besides their technical or operational task assignments.

"Benedict pointed out that societies that had social orders in which the individual by the same act and at the same time served his own advantage and that of the group were characterized by a low incidence of aggressive behavior" (Marmor 1974, p. 422). The reason was not that people were entirely unselfish but merely that societal institutions provided enough flexibility for personal desires to coincide with social obligations. Therefore, aggressive behavior was not provoked by societal tasks because it was unnecessary. Benedict (1934) distinguished between "high synergy" and "low synergy" cultures, defining the latter as societies where "the advantage of one individual was generally at the expense of another and thus intrasocial competitiveness was fostered" (Marmor 1974, p. 422). From these studies she found that emotional security appeared to be more important than the distribution of wealth.

Part of this concept can be applied to organizations if it is kept in mind that the synergy level depends on different variables. Dealing with organizations never becomes a depersonalized abstract pattern for the psychiatrist. By contrast, however, economic and sociological approaches have become more mechanical and less personal. Approaches based on abstract research, economic data, statistical surveys, and structural analysis by management consultants have not only failed to recognize human needs but in some cases have led to serious distress and more disorganization. The human capacity to adapt to rapid changes, the unconscious resistances to change, the deterioration of informal communication, the tolerance for tension, and the unconscious need for security were underestimated resulting in more organizational dysfunction.

The search for remedies and the uncritical application of various encounter group methods have created a phony atmosphere of pseudo-instant intimacy. The often desperate need for unreflected action without diagnosis has contributed to many symptoms of organizational dysfunction such as high turnover rates (especially among the younger generation), increasing absenteeism, illness, alcoholism, and inappropriate social behavior, as well as costly production failure rates, recalls, or decreases in quality. These functional or dysfunctional results can be left to neighboring disciplines as long as they are willing to recognize that the neglected human factor, the psychology of well-being, and the need for effective methods of mental health maintenance are at the bottom of these symptoms of organizational dysfunction. It is necessary to stress the importance of human factors which are often considered the unwanted by-product of successful operations in business, government, and community institutions.

The increasing divorce rate among police officers, the escalating political violence, the struggle to control school systems, the growing alcoholism in industry and business, more frequent coronary attacks and psychosomatic illness among top executives can no longer be ascribed exclusively to individual intrapsychic conflict. The impact of organizational conditions and structures might cause a high percentage of these allegedly individual symptoms, although many of these symptoms are also connected with changing societal values and attitudes as well as with increasing collective fears.

The challenge of these problems to the psychiatrist has its counterpart in the law. The law enforcement officer must wait until a criminal act has been committed although he might have foreknowledge that a crime will be committed. No law permits interference with personal rights. This example is a striking instance of an institutionalized ideology that has developed an independent autonomy because the formal organizational conditions are perceived as representing a higher value than human needs. The law becomes an abstract pattern which the individual automatically follows regardless of the destructive results.

Psychiatry is in danger of restricting itself in a similar way to an erroneous medical model which fails to interfere and apply its knowledge as long as no illness can be defined. Scheff (1966) describes the physician's dilemma by distinguishing two alternatives: (1) Nobody should be treated who is not sick; (2) no illness should be overlooked. Both contradicting principles are applied differently depending upon conditions. During a war or emergency, illness is not defined the same way as it is during better times. In the affluent society diagnostic methods are intensified because no illness is overlooked as long as costs permit extensive diagnosis. The process reverses itself during wars or catastrophies when even sick people are used for emergency, maintenance, or defense services. Thus, we can observe the impact of changing value systems on diagnostic criteria. These standards depend upon the environmental circumstances and human needs as well as on the autonomy of institutions which develop a life of their own once they have been formed. The autonomous institution can force the individual professional to become a servant of institutional maintenance.

Most organizations know that some important factors are lacking within their conventional economic and technical structures. Many organizations have begun to recognize the serious complaints of their leading executives who claimed that the traditional annual health checkup never solved their problem of critically assessing their lives and family situations as well as their personal future. The medical model rarely recognizes psychological problems as signs of real beginning illness. However, we know from Menninger et al. (1963) as well as from Selye's (1956) research on stress that illness as defined in medicine has various premorbid stages. One of the first stages is psychological stress which leads to functional symptoms and finally to organic illness if the internal psychological conflicts are not solved. The diagnostic question to be answered in the future deals with the crucial problem of the extent to which organizations impose conditions on individuals which lead to psychological stress and consequently to vital decompensations, dysfunctions, or illnesses.

Returning to the question about the adequacy of the traditional medical model, I want to point out the importance of developing new methods for organizational diagnosis through a multidisciplinary approach. The organizational climate is only one variable in determining the chances for the maintenance of mental health or destructive decompensation and illness. In the past there have been various psychiatric efforts to apply to organizations untenable generalizations from individual psychiatry or personality theory. These trial and error periods have made it more difficult to arrive at a different approach safeguarded from such oversimplifications. The whole scientific theory of organizations is full of traps and pitfalls as long as we assume one discipline can solve all the existing problems. In a multidisciplinary group approach, sociological, economic, psychological, and psychosocial data would be cross-examined by various disciplines, each dealing with specific problems of individual relationships within organizations. The psychiatrist in such a multidisciplinary team would be forced to know more about sociology, anthropology, psychology, and applied psychoanalysis as well as about technical, economic, and structural management conditions. Knowledge from a variety of disciplines enables the psychiatrist to tailor his diagnosis to help the organization's leaders who are often without appropriate knowledge of how to implement those changes that are highly dependent on the human factor.

A short but rather typical example may demonstrate the necessity of having a psychiatrist on the team making the diagnosis and the suggestions for resolving existing organizational problems. A well-known management consultant firm completed a major survey of a large business and advised the organization to change its basic structure from being headed by an executive committee to being headed by two elected individuals—a chairman of the board and a president. This new leadership structure was announced to the organization's top executives in a forty-five minute session without any further comment; the meeting was concluded with, "That's it—any questions?" Although there was an increasing level of anxiety, no questions were asked. This change put the majority of vice-presidents on a lower level and required them to deal individually with either one of the leaders, who were rarely present at the same time but substituted for each other. Within a few months serious infighting, dysfunctioning, uncertainty, and depression developed within the group of vice-presidents. Their reactions had dysfunctional repercussions throughout the organization. The negative consequences of this recommended structural change are apparent. The organizational diagnosis oriented primarily toward evaluating economic and management data failed because the importance of human psychological needs was completely overlooked.

Space does not permit other examples, but additional evidence would only strengthen the conclusion that the most important factor in organizational diagnosis is the exploration of relationships within organizations and the discovery of hidden agendas among top-level managers. The hierarchy and the relationship between vice-presidents, department heads, or various secondary "alpha functions" determine the basic organizational climate and create within the majority of "gamma functions" either trust and willingness to follow or develop instead distrust, opposition, and use of "omega functions" by "gamma functions" as destructive weapons against "alpha functions." The voice of the "beta function" within organizations is usually ignored until the "omega" parts of the organization are presented as more and more dangerous symptoms threatening to deskill or paralyze the leading "alphas" who then tend to scapegoat the "omega function." Once we have identified the units or subunits of a larger system, we can return to the question of whether there are any coping mechanisms of organizations analogous to those of persons.

It must be kept in mind that any analogy between an abstract organization and an individual will fail because an organization as an entity per se would not or could not exist without persons who by their individual actions and decisions determine the organization's goals and directions. It is the individual motivation for implementing, avoiding, procrastinating, or delegating decisions within the organization's hierarchy of families that determines organizational functioning. These individual factors are necessary basic information for organizational diagnosis. The various individual defense mechanisms and object relations of persons in "alpha" positions also determine whether the organization is perceived as an autonomous entity demanding each individual to serve a maintenance function or as an interchangeable wheel, or whether the organization can create a high synergy level by providing the individual functions that benefit the person as well as the group or organization in the same act. Job satisfaction, group solidarity, feelings of well-being and belonging, and the development of a genuine identity depend on this primary choice. This goal involves not only the work satisfaction of employees but also their family relations and their private lives.

We are entering the *terra incognita* of psychiatry and psychology. The natural reaction is to stay out of this dangerous new territory which seems full of traps and pitfalls. However, we must explore new diagnostic frontiers because neither the sociological nor the economic approaches have penetrated the darkness of this unknown territory. Psychiatry and psychoanalysis are under attack because they withdrew from the main societal and social problems and instead focused on individual treatment. The psychiatrist claims to be the advocate of reality for his patient who tries to escape into a private world of delusions or infantile dreams. However, since more than sixty percent of the people in Western civilizations spend a minimum of eight hours per day working for some kind of organization, we cannot retreat into a professional dream world where psychiatrists only diagnose the solitary patient. We must face the real problems of organizations and answer some basic questions such as: What are organizations doing to people? Can we prevent the autonomous organization from usurping the individual? Can we stop organizational autonomy? But before answering these questions, we must decide how much of our own professional intention is biased by organizational prejudice. Martin Buber (1949) reminds us of the first step to knowledge when he considers the reaction of the first man to the voice of God calling, "Adam, where are you?" We cannot attempt a single solution to the problems of organizational diagnosis if, like Adam, we are found hiding.

References

ASCH, S. E.: Studies in the Principles of Judgments and Attitudes: II. Determination of Judgments by Group and by Ego Standards. *J. Soc. Psychol.* 12:431–65, 1940.

———: Effects of Group Pressure Upon the Modification and Distortion of Judgments. In *Groups, Leadership and Men: Research in Human Relations*, H. S. Guetzkow, ed. Pittsburgh: Carnegie Press, 1951.

———: *Social Psychology.* New York: Prentice-Hall, 1952.

BENEDICT, RUTH: *Patterns of Culture.* Boston: Houghton Mifflin, 1934.

BION, W. R.: Experiences in Groups, I. *Human Relations* 1(3):314–20, 1948a.

———: Experiences in Groups, II. *Human Relations* 1(4):487–96, 1948b.

————: Experiences in Groups, III. *Human Relations* 2(1):13–22, 1949a.
————: Experiences in Groups, IV. *Human Relations* 2(4):295–303, 1949b.
————: Experiences in Groups, V. *Human Relations* 3(1):3–14, 1950a.
————: Experiences in Groups, VI. *Human Relations* 3(4):395–402, 1950b.
————: Group Dynamics: A Re-View. *Int. J. Psychoanal.* 33(2):235–47, 1952.
BROCHER, TOBIAS et al.: *Study of Private Business Sector Involvement in Community Intervention.* Topeka: Center for Applied Behavioral Sciences, The Menninger Foundation, 1975 (unpublished).
BUBER, MARTIN: *Die Erzaehlungen Der Chassidim.* Zurich: Manesse Verlag, 1949.
CARTWRIGHT, D. P. & ZANDER, ALVIN, eds.: *Group Dynamics: Research & Theory.* Evanston, IL: Row, Peterson, 1960.
FREUD, SIGMUND (1921): Group Psychology and the Analysis of the Ego. *Standard Edition* 18:69–143, 1955.
GOULDNER, A. W.: Explorations in Applied Social Science. In *Applied Sociology: Opportunities and Problems,* A. W. Gouldner & S. M. Miller, eds., pp. 5–22. New York: Free Press, 1965.
GREEN, ALVIN et al.: *Study of Community Intervention.* Topeka: Department of Preventive Psychiatry, The Menninger Foundation, 1972 (unpublished).
JANIS, E. L.: *Psychological Stress: Psychoanalytic and Behavioral Studies of Surgical Patients.* New York: Wiley, 1958.
JAQUES, ELLIOTT: *Equitable Payment.* New York: Wiley, 1961.
KUHN, ALFRED: *The Logic of Social Systems: A Unified, Deductive, System-Based Approach to Social Science.* San Francisco: Jossey-Bass, 1974.
LEWIN, KURT: Field Theory. In *Social Science: Selected Theoretical Papers,* D. P. Cartwright, ed. New York: Harper, 1951.
LEWIN, KURT et al.: Patterns of Aggressive Behavior in Experimentally Created Social Climates. *J. Soc. Psychol.* 10:271–99, 1939.
MARMOR, JUDD: *Psychiatry in Transition: Selected Papers of Judd Marmor, M.D.* New York: Brunner/Mazel, 1974.
MENNINGER, KARL et al.: *The Vital Balance.* New York: Viking Press, 1963.
MENNINGER, W. C.: Psychiatric Experiences in the War, 1941–1946. *Am. J. Psychiatry* 103(3):577–86, 1947.
MILGRAM, S.: Some Conditions of Obedience and Disobedience to Authority. *Human Relations* 18(1):57–76, 1965.
NEFF, F. W.: Survey Research: A Tool for Problem Diagnosis and Improvement in Organizations. In *Applied Sociology: Opportunities and Problems,* A. W. Gouldner & S. M. Miller, eds., pp. 23–38. New York: Free Press, 1965.
SATTEN, JOSEPH et al.: *Study of Community Intervention.* Topeka: Department of Preventive Psychiatry, The Menninger Foundation, 1970–71 (unpublished).
SCHEFF, T. J.: *Being Mentally Ill: A Sociological Theory.* Chicago: Aldine, 1966.
SELYE, HANS: *The Stress of Life.* New York: McGraw-Hill, 1956.
SHERIF, MUZAFER: *The Psychology of Social Norms.* New York: Harper & Row, 1966.
SHERIF, MUZAFER & SHERIF, CAROLYN: *Groups in Harmony and Tension: An Integration of Studies of Intergroup Relations.* New York: Harper & Bros., 1953.
SHERIF, MUZAFER et al.: Status in Experimentally Produced Groups. *Am. J. Sociol.* 60(4):370–79, 1955.

DIAGNOSIS OF CULTURE AND SOCIAL INSTITUTIONS

ROY W. MENNINGER, M.D.*

A discussion of diagnosis in relation to culture and social institutions is a logical extension of our conference topic, but it is a
task more properly suited to an anthropologist or a sociologist than
to a psychiatrist. So, instead, I would like to examine several issues
in our own social institution of medicine. Perhaps a look at these
issues, embedded as they are in our culture, could be considered
a kind of diagnostic inquiry.

These several issues have deep roots in Western thinking, and
in fact are conceptual backbones in much of our medical practice.
They are more important now, and perhaps more of an issue now,
because the public's expectations of physicians and medicine have
been changing so rapidly, creating new problems for us as well as
for our patients, that it is now necessary for us to take a fresh
look at what we do as physicians and how we define disease, health,
medical practice—yes, even psychiatry. Important as these issues
are for organizing much of Western medical philosophy, they also
represent barriers to the development of an integrated medicine: a
perspective of the person which links both mind and body, and
health and sickness.

These paired words—mind/body, health/sickness—imply polarities and, in that mode, represent splits or extremes along several
continua. As physicians we speak of uniting mind and body in

---

* President, The Menninger Foundation, Topeka, Kansas.

our practice (psychiatrists, in particular, talk that way), yet there are few physicians indeed who give equal importance and attention to *both* mind and body. We speak of health as a significant medical objective, yet the establishment of a disease-free state more accurately describes the aim of most physicians, as if health and the absence of disease were synonymous.

In reality these polarities are united more in medical rhetoric than in medical practice. Most physicians have in fact settled to one side or the other of each polarity—some considerably farther and more entrenched than others. They have forsaken the task of reconciling these polarities, leaving that task to medical philosophers in order to get on with the work of taking care of the sick. Unfortunately, the "sick" who seek help are not so clear about which end of these continua they are on: What they know is that they hurt, they grieve, they are anxious, they are in pain; they do not immediately presume it is all physical or all mental; they are not always sure when they are sick and when they are healthy. For most patients, as indeed for most of us as individual persons, mind and body are indistinguishably intertwined. For physicians, mind and body are separated only by the rather arbitrary perspectives we have learned to use in our examination of the patients who come to us.

It is apparent that these separations of mind from body, of sickness from health, substantially simplify a great many problems (the scope of any particular specialty of medicine, what should be taught and by whom, and so forth), though at the cost of fragmenting the patient, and failing to deal adequately with the whole of the problem he brings. A surgeon, for example, may deal fully with the physiological and pathological problems of creating a coronary bypass, and ignore or dismiss the major depression which has developed.

Reconciliation of these polarities is made difficult by the fact that each end of the continuum has developed quite separate thought systems which in turn are predicated on quite different assumptions about the nature of man. Underlying the body focus is a physicochemical concept of life derived from nineteenth century science. Dynamic psychiatry on the other hand has developed from metaphorical roots into complex sets of abstractions, initially finding more in common with religious thought than with medicine or science. Each system in turn has emphasized internal consistency at the expense of its relations to sectors of knowledge beyond its boundaries. In a predictable way, each system has perceived the other as different, therefore extraneous and irrelevant. Even dynamic psychiatry often appears to consider the body as little more than a vehicle for carrying the mind—a viewpoint quite similar to that of the internist or surgeon who regards the body as a place where the disease is, and the mind as irrelevant. Again, the patients who are caught in between make a far less precise and convenient split: the fearful cardiac or surgical patient whose apprehension precipitates his death on the operating table; or the disease-prone, helpless, hopeless patient whose giving up precipitates illness; or the hospitalized child. These patients are clearly involved in *both* mind and body, but upon reflection, is not everyone?

In regard to the second polarity, health/sickness, medical philosophy is more ambivalent. Health is generally regarded as an uncontestable good, yet as already suggested, the average physician does not make health (in the broader, World Health Organization definition) his objective. The general assumption that health is or results from the absence of disease is widespread, in psychiatry as well as in general medicine. I would like to quote from a colleague who has written on the issues of life goals and treatment goals, and speaks specifically of this issue:

> Mental illness may be looked upon as an interruption and a distortion of developmental processes. Psychoanalysis is a treatment method that aims at the removal of the causes of such an interruption so that development can be resumed. If this treatment goal is achieved it makes it possible for the patient to reach his life goals. A clinical distinction between treatment goals and life goals is important for the conduct of therapy, and this can be done despite their partial overlap. *Life goals* are the goals the patient would seek to attain if he could put his potentialities to use. In other words, they are the goals this patient would aim at if his 'true self' . . . and his creativity were free. Treatment goals concern the removal of obstacles to the patient's discovery of what his potentialities are [Ticho 1972, p. 315].

This rather Rousseauian idea is an idealistic version of what happens once obstacles are removed from what is presumed to be a normal developmental course. One might wonder whether in fact that necessarily happens. Is health so automatic?

The necessity of combining the teaching of new or different life styles, conflict management techniques, sources of gratification, work skills, etc. with therapy, even for the moderately ill psychiatric patient, suggests that successful (healthful) living requires additional skills, knowledge, or even experiences beyond those interventions of the psychiatrist strictly described as therapy. Similar parallels exist for the physically ill patient: Healthful living requires explicit strategies for achieving it and does not automatically happen at the conclusion of surgery or course of penicillin.

Moreover, the lack of much attention to health as a legitimate and significant focus of the practicing physician means that prevention is ignored altogether or left to the school nurse, the physical education teacher, the dental technician. Though it is accurate to note that the general physician feels overwhelmed now with responsibilities for handling the sick without the additional burden of maintaining the well person's health, this feeling perpetuates the artificial division between these interconnected states of being.

Contemporary conditions of change have begun to make it harder and harder to sustain both the mind/body split and the health/illness split. In the first place, there are increasing evidences of intimate relationships between mind and body. So far the information is fragmented and piecemeal, and not yet a part of either theoretical system. But experimental as well as clinical evidence suggests that the condition of one will have effects on the state of the other. This fact is not news to us as evident in earlier interests in conditions we characterized as "psychosomatic," acknowledging the fact that somehow mind and body were connected though we knew not how. And from this rather awkward terminologic union we have begun to move toward the conception that mind and body do, in fact, operate in a common and a scientific acknowledgment of experiential unity in every one of us. Each of us is very much aware that our body and our mind are closely connected though this intimate knowledge dissolves when we shift our attention to our patients. There are, moreover, too many noncategorizable conditions that do not fit either health or illness, nor do they belong to either mind or body alone.

Consider such phenomena as faith healing or voodoo death, or the poignant instance of a husband whose wife of thirty-five years dies and three weeks later he is dead of a "broken heart." Yet the *Diagnostic and Statistical Manual* has no entry for broken hearts. Or consider the variety of physical symptoms that express symbolic conflict or an effort to resolve it—backaches and headaches—or even exclusively psychological symptoms which have a curious relationship to physical disease. I think of a patient Dr. Kübler-Ross (1973) describes so eloquently—a woman who had terminal cancer and had been totally rejected by her husband as an insufferable, impossible person. He was glad to confine her to the hospital. Even the hospital ward attendants and nurses had difficulty dealing with her, so they put her out of the way in the very end room and seldom visited her. When Dr. Ross went into this stuffy room, so negligently maintained, she found this woman with a smile on her face. Waving her arms, and pointing to the bare walls and the sterile appearance of the room, she said, "Aren't the flowers beautiful?" Rather than rushing to the window to open it for air which the room badly needed, Dr. Ross acknowledged that the (nonexistent) flowers were indeed beautiful. The point of the story is that psychic hallucinations clearly had a vital role in maintaining this woman's psychological integrity in the face of physical disease. To call this symptom simply evidence of mental illness would have been to misread the significance of it in her own biological and psychological economy.

Cultural changes are also making it harder to maintain these splits. Affluence has made people increasingly comfortable physically. They have time now to ask questions that go beyond essential requirements for food and for shelter, questions having to do with meaning and satisfaction and fulfillment—questions they sometimes ask of their physicians, and often of their psychiatrists. These questions are not adequately encompassed by the splits between mind/body and health/illness. I wonder if the escalation in our material and physical achievements has created an escalation of our psychological expectations as well. With our capacity to improve ourselves in so many physical ways, is it not encouraging us to ask progressively more difficult questions about new levels of psychological adjustment and experience?

Our technological successes imply a potential for equivalent success in the psychological sphere, yet they permit us to draw some sharp contrasts: We have the capacity to go to the moon, but we do not dare go to the corner after dark; we have the capacity to design critical machines of destruction, but we do not apply this capacity to the development of social systems that will make the use of destructive weaponry unnecessary. To all of these pressures there are obvious dramatic responses—the tremendous upsurge of the counterculture movement and the human potential movement is impressive, offering the possibility of guilt-free pleasure.

It seems fair to say that traditional medicine—at least a medicine that practices these splits of mind/body and health/illness—is on a collision course with some of the newer approaches and newer concepts about the nature of man and the nature of man's needs, for pressures to value the maintenance of health as highly as the treatment of disease and the interactive influences of mind and body are mounting. They cannot be ignored. What is not clear at this point is whether medicine with its limiting conceptions of disease and health and of mind and body will accommodate to this confrontation by growing and changing, or whether the inevitable resistances will reject these perspectives and thereby abandon them to exploitation by charlatans and faddists. I think medicine is going to be faced with increasing demands from consumers that greater attention be paid to the *person* who lives in the body, to his world view, his emotional states, his relationships—in short, his health—and not merely to the disease he is alleged to have.

It seems obvious at this point that people are expecting considerably more than cure. There is a hungry need for something to fill a deep void; there is a dawning recognition that we are open systems and capable of growth and change long after childhood and adolescence. We are adaptive learning systems, and as such it ought to be possible for us, as Karl and Will Menninger have said, to become "weller than well." But the question is whether American medicine will rise to this challenge and accept the possibility that these redefinitions can be constructive and enlarged upon, or whether instead we will retract and retreat.

Right now the possibilities of the former are not bright. This is in part because the doctor has too much narcissistic investment in his power position vis-à-vis the patient. Many of us have developed subtle but disguised ways of maintaining that power position, all in the name of "good treatment." The fact is that medicine, as many of us practice it, encourages a patient's dependency. It does not encourage a more desirable goal, namely the establishment of a kind of parity in the relationship that promotes a greater responsibility by the patient for his own treatment. It is interesting to see how some experiences in this direction—e.g., biofeedback with alcoholics—have illustrated to the patient that he has, in fact, some capacity to control himself and perhaps by extension some capacity to control his disorder. Physicians generally do not give enough attention to the need for enabling, encouraging, promoting patients to establish a greater sense of individual control, a sense of mastery, through a kind of therapeutic alliance rather than a therapeutic autocracy that is psychologically and economically gratifying to the physician. I am well aware that our patients are expert at putting us in a position narcissistically satisfying to us, making it thereby more difficult to recognize this problem and to change it. Furthermore, it is unlikely that physicians will be willing to give up their superior economic and political positions; it is quite likely that we will, if necessary, define disease more and more narrowly, more and more precisely, and more and more "scientifically," in order to be sure that what remains is clearly under our control. Witness the recent example of an attempt to define "medical psychotherapy," a clear indication, by inference at least, that psychotherapy of a medical kind is different from psychotherapy of a nonmedical kind—one kind practiced by physicians and another kind practiced by others.

Consider also the surprising shift by the American Psychiatric Association to a closer relationship with the American Medical Association. It does not seem probable that this shift is because the two organizations have suddenly discovered much in common in their social philosophies; it is more likely a reflection of political reality. The American Medical Association maintains a more powerful, better paid lobby in Washington than the psychiatrists do. But the alliance of the two organizations increases the probability that we will see narrower definitions of what mental illness is, with progressive limits to what might be called essentially biochemical and biological definitions of disease.

Such reactionary narrowing of the scope of our business brings to mind the nearly disastrous experiences of the railroads, so well described by Levitt (1975). He notes that their progressive deterioration, due to a steady decrease in the number of customers, was not because the need for passenger and freight transportation declined or because the need for transportation was filled by others, but because it was not filled by the railroads themselves. They allowed others to take customers away from them because they defined their business too narrowly—as railroads in the sense of pieces of real estate with steel rails and box cars rolling on them— rather than realizing that they should have moved toward the broad, expansionistic opportunities of the transportation business. Their limited perspective not only permitted them to overlook valuable opportunities but bound them to a reactionary point of view that could not change with the times.

In like fashion, we physicians must not make the mistake of narrowly defining the nature of our business at a time when the consumer appears to be demanding more than simply curing a disease. We must become more adaptive. To begin with we can acknowledge that there is more in this world than we understand and more that we need to know, and we can work to retain this humility. We need to reaccept the whole person, not simply allowing the body to remain in the province of one group of physicians while the mind is off with another. Perhaps we need to examine more carefully and learn from some of the self-improvement techniques so popular today: the biogenic approaches to healing including biofeedback, the Silva mind control technique, acupuncture, the Erhard Seminar Training programs, and transcendental meditation, to name a few. We must resist the short-term comforts of orthodoxy lest we discover that its limitations have become prison walls that will isolate us still further. An unsatisfied clientele may likely search elsewhere—the needs and the pressures for fulfilling them being what they are. It is notable that only a few physicians are working within the counterculture of healing activities. Unfortunately, I think this failure to engage in some of these newer forms of treatment may lead to a chauvinistic defensive stance on our part. We would then certainly be open to the charge —medicine as well as psychiatry—that we are more interested in protecting our turf than in protecting our patients.

Lest I seem to be aiming my remarks exclusively at medicine and psychiatry, I should add that I think the human potential movement suffers from some of the same problems. It, too, needs to engage in a careful, thoughtful examination of psychological phenomena and attempt to understand them. Right now the human potential movement appears to be such a solipsistic, anti-intellectual bunch of arrogant people, all operating in the name of humanism, that it is hard to see how intellectual activities of the sort I feel are so necessary could ever prosper, let alone begin. A perspective that assumes feeling is everything and thought is only epiphenomenal, an obstacle to human well-being, can hardly be expected to advance knowledge. We have to be prepared to study human experiences and examine them, and to the extent that such a group makes this task impossible, it postpones bringing together the several splits to which I have referred.

One final point: We do not now have a conceptual system that will accommodate data from these various sources to produce an integrated or coordinated perspective. I am proud of the fact that at the Menninger Foundation we have begun such an effort by examining some of these approaches through a psychoanalytic conceptual framework in an effort to understand and integrate psychological knowledge (Appelbaum 1976). This work underscores the importance of dialogue—discussion not simply between psychiatrists and others involved in the newer forms of treatment, but among ourselves as well. Inevitably this dialogue will take the form of a dialectic, making clear the importance of developing a tolerance for the consequent conflict. To acknowledge differences is not to take sides or to make moral judgments, but to promote truth. No one has a corner on truth, least of all the zealot who insists on it. As we have seen, attitudes toward the body have changed, attitudes toward medicine and within medicine have changed, and there will still be further changes. But some universal values unique to man are independent of these cycles of history.

The need to retain this broader perspective was eloquently summarized by Reinhold Niebuhr (1952):

> Nothing that is worth doing can be achieved in our lifetime; therefore we must be saved by hope. Nothing which is true or beautiful or good makes complete sense in any immediate context of history; therefore we must be saved by faith. Nothing we do, however virtuous, can be accomplished alone; therefore we are saved by love [p. 63].

References

APPELBAUM, STEPHEN A.: Introduction. In *The Only Dance There Is* by Ram Dass. New York: Jason Aronson, 1976.

KÜBLER-ROSS, ELISABETH: *Lessons from the Dying Patient.* Audiotaped (5 cassettes). The Author, 1973.

LEVITT, THEODORE: Marketing Myopia. *Harvard Business Review*, Sept.–Oct. 1975, pp. 26ff.

NIEBUHR, REINHOLD: *The Irony of American History.* New York: Charles Scribner's Sons, 1952.

TICHO, E. A.: Termination of Psychoanalysis: Treatment Goals, Life Goals. *Psychoanal. Q.* 41(3):315–33, 1972.

Special Diagnostic
Perspectives and Situations

DIAGNOSIS IN PLANNING
PSYCHOPHARMACOLOGICAL THERAPY

FRANK J. AYD, JR., M.D.*

It is often alleged that the advent of the psychopharmaceuticals has made the task of the psychiatrist much easier; that all the psychiatrist has to do is know which target symptoms are relieved by which drugs and prescribe accordingly. No longer does he have to be an astute clinical observer, a careful, thorough history compiler, an able diagnostician, or a knowledgeable expert about the natural clinical course of psychiatric illnesses. In short, the psychiatrist no longer has to be a physician but can be solely a pill dispenser.

As a staunch advocate of rational psychopharmacotherapy, I disagree completely with all these allegations. I am firmly convinced that mastering the art of using these medicines effectively, safely, and economically requires that the physician-prescriber be a skilled clinician, adept in history taking, and capable of making reasonably precise psychiatric diagnoses, including an assessment of the patient's basic personality. Furthermore, the physician-prescriber must be knowledgeable about the patient's physical status, aware of his family and personal drug histories, and well acquainted

---

* Director, Professional Education and Research, Taylor Manor Hospital, Ellicott City, Maryland.

with the clinical indications, contraindications, dosages, and pharmacological and toxicological properties of the various psychoactive drugs. Finally, since the physician-prescriber is not simply treating an illness but a human being who has an illness, it is imperative he acknowledge that all patients require not just a drug but also compassion, understanding, an attentive ear, counseling, support, and some degree of formal psychotherapy in order to achieve optimal therapeutic results. Additionally, since no man is an island, those who come within the sphere of the patient's influence also may have to be included in the total treatment program. Hence, relative to the individual patient and the nature of his specific psychiatric disorder, psychopharmacotherapy often must be carried out conjointly not only with individual psychotherapy but with group therapy, family therapy, behavior modification, and possibly other therapies.

If a physician is to fulfill a patient's moral and legal right to effective, safe, and economical psychopharmacotherapy, it is imperative that he make as accurate a psychiatric diagnosis as possible before he writes a prescription for a psychoactive compound. There are many reasons for this dictum. The psychopharmaceuticals we have at our disposal, because of their diverse actions in the central nervous system, often have more than one clinical indication. But the members of the different groups of psychopharmaceuticals—neuroleptics, lithium, tricyclic antidepressants, the monoamine oxidase inhibitors, and the so-called minor tranquilizers—also have specific clinical indications and, when properly prescribed, are capable of producing desirable therapeutic results. On the other hand, when prescribed for illnesses for which these compounds are not specifically indicated, not only is their therapeutic efficacy likely to be less than optimal, but the prospects of undesirable effects are enhanced.

Neuroleptics, for example, are the drugs of choice for the treatment of schizophrenia. This finding has been verified repeatedly by controlled and uncontrolled clinical trials throughout the world. Lithium, by contrast, has been proven through stringently controlled trials to be the drug of choice for mania and hypomania. Neuroleptics can be used to treat mania and hypomania but the therapeutic results are due not to specific antimanic effects, but to their nonspecific sedative effects. Lithium has a specific nonsedative effect on the psychopathology and pathophysiology of mania and hypomania but does not have the antipsychotic effects of the neuroleptics in schizophrenic illnesses.

Distinguishing between schizophrenia and manic depressive psychosis is not always easy, but making such a differential diagnosis is mandatory before either a neuroleptic or lithium is prescribed. Unfortunately, making this differential diagnosis is not done currently as often as it should be. Consequently there are schizophrenic illnesses being treated with lithium because they have been misdiagnosed manic depressive, and manic depressive illnesses being treated with neuroleptics because they have been misdiagnosed schizophrenic.

These diagnostic and secondary therapeutic errors account not only for poor therapeutic outcomes but, equally important, they are responsible for a rise in the incidence of serious complications due to lithium and neuroleptics. Metabolically, there are major differences between schizophrenic and manic depressive patients. These differences influence how the victims of these disorders react to the drugs administered to them. Manic patients, for example, have a greater tolerance for lithium than schizophrenic patients. On the other hand, schizophrenic patients have a greater tolerance for neuroleptics than do manic depressive patients. Consequently, schizophrenic patients not only are not as therapeutically responsive to lithium as manic depressive patients, but are more vulnerable to developing lithium intoxication and for aggravating their schizophrenic illness. Manic depressive patients, as I mentioned, not only are not as responsive to neuroleptics as they are to lithium, but they risk developing neuroleptic-induced extrapyramidal reactions, including tardive dyskinesia.

Since I have stressed the value of lithium compared to neuroleptics in the treatment of mania and hypomania, I must point out that lithium is not as effective an antidepressant as are the tricyclic antidepressants. But lithium has compelled psychiatrists to be more precise diagnosticians—the current classification of manic depressives into bipolar and unipolar types is due chiefly to the advent of lithium and the therapeutic results it produces. Lithium is most valuable for the treatment of bipolar manic depressive patients, preventing or minimizing recurrent episodes of elation. Lithium also may prevent or minimize recurrent attacks of depression in both bipolar and unipolar manic depressives, particularly in the bipolar; but once a bipolar or unipolar type becomes depressed, lithium is not effective as an antidepressant. Clearly, therefore, before lithium is prescribed, a physician must make a definitive diagnosis to avoid misprescribing this drug. The physician must realize that the more truly manic or hypomanic the patient is, the better the therapeutic results are likely to be, and that in patients not truly manic or hypomanic, the therapeutic results will be poorer.

Although neuroleptics can be and have been used to treat depression, especially agitated depression with or without paranoid features, they are not as specific or as efficacious as the tricyclic antidepressants in the treatment of unipolar and bipolar manic depressive patients. Neuroleptics do not affect mood as the tricyclics do. Hence, for the treatment of depression, tricyclic antidepressants are the drugs of choice, providing it is the illness depression and not the symptom depression for which tricyclics are prescribed.

The vital importance of distinguishing between the illness depression and the symptom depression before prescribing a tricyclic antidepressant cannot be overstressed. Because this differential diagnosis is not often made, many patients and physicians are unhappy and disgruntled with a medication that instead of allowing the patient to feel better makes him feel worse because of the side effects it produces. Just as there is a metabolic difference between schizophrenic patients and manic depressive patients which accounts for the differences in their responses to lithium and neuroleptics, so too are there important metabolic differences between patients with the illness depression and those with the symptom depression. These differences account for the various therapeutic responses to and tolerance for tricyclic antidepressants. Therefore, patients with the illness depression are candidates for tricyclic antidepressant therapy; patients with the symptom depression should not be treated with tricyclic antidepressants.

The physician must remember the crucial lesson Kuhn* taught when he first demonstrated the efficacy of the tricyclics, namely

---

* Kuhn, R.: The Treatment of Depressive States with an Iminodibenzyl Derivative (G 22355). *Schweiz. med. Wschr.* 87:1135, 1957.

that the patient who is the best candidate for these drugs must have what Kuhn calls a "vital" depression by which he means a pure classical melancholia. Such a patient responds optimally to appropriate tricyclic antidepressant drug therapy, whereas the less pure a depression is, the poorer are the therapeutic results.

Another group of antidepressant drugs is the monoamine oxidase inhibitors (MAOs). Their mode of action is different from and they do not have exactly the same clinical indications as the tricyclic antidepressants. It is true that MAOs are antidepressants, but their efficacy in pure endogenous or "vital" depression appears to be not as good as the therapeutic efficacy of the tricyclic antidepressants. This result may be due to genetic factors. Pharmacogenetic data indicate that manic depressive patients may be subdivided into those responsive to either a tricyclic alone or an MAO alone. This point is just one of the many good reasons why a physician should take a family and a personal drug history before he prescribes a psychopharmaceutical.

One type of affective disorder for which MAOs often are the drugs of choice is what is frequently labeled an *atypical depression*. It occurs most often in the middle-aged, especially women, who besides being depressed also manifest a variety of hysterical symptoms. These patients, in contrast to patients with an endogenous depression, seldom have severe anorexia or insomnia characterized by early morning awakening, nor do they reveal any significant psychomotor retardation. Instead, they sob hysterically, often are agitated, eat reasonably well, maintain their weight, and once asleep remain so until morning. They are phobic and detest all sedative drugs. If they have ever had electroconvulsive therapy, they swear that it produced permanent memory loss. Some of these patients respond favorably to a tricyclic antidepressant but the majority respond optimally more quickly, often within a week to ten days, to an MAO.

Besides making as accurate a psychiatric diagnosis as possible and carefully distinguishing the various forms of depression from each other as well as from drug-induced depression or from physical disorders such as hypothyroidism, a physician should know the patient's basic personality structure. This information can play an influential role in the outcome of psychopharmacotherapy. For example, patients with obsessive personalities detest and will not take psychoactive drugs that are strongly sedative and therefore interfere with their self-imposed standards. If such patients are given a sedative drug, they often become quite anxious and complain that they feel as if they were in a chemical straitjacket from which they secure release by either stopping the medicine or by reducing the dose to a therapeutically ineffective level. Also they often compromise therapeutic outcome in other ways. Some are do-it-yourself physicians, taking medicines not as prescribed but according to their own personal criteria. Some reason that if two doses are good, then three or four will be better and medicate themselves accordingly. Others, because of a phobia about becoming dependent or addicted, take less than the prescribed dosage. Still others are so rigid that they scrupulously adhere to the prescription directions. If they are told to take medicine after meals and if for any reason they miss a meal, they will not take the medicine. These few illustrations should convince the physician that he must know not only what illness he is prescribing for, but also who has the illness.

I have stressed that a family history and a personal drug history should be taken before writing a prescription for a psychoactive drug. This information should be as comprehensive as possible and from the patient it should include all recently ingested medicines, including over-the-counter remedies. Pharmacogenetic data now available indicate that responsiveness, refractoriness, dosage requirements, and side effects are quite similar among first-degree blood relatives. A personal drug history may allow the physician not only to make the clinical diagnosis but to select a preferable pharmacotherapy as well. Many patients are unbelievable drug consumers and a personal drug history may provide the true explanation for the patient's psychopathology.

Clearly a physician must choose from the range of available compounds those which would be best for the individual patient in view of his illness, his personality, his physical status, his family and personal drug histories. The physician is treating not just an illness but a human being with an illness. Hence, the physician must diagnose the total person and then select the psychoactive compound based on its pharmacological properties. The importance of the physician knowing the pharmacological properties of psychoactive compounds cannot be overemphasized.

Having selected a particular psychoactive drug for a patient, the physician's next task is to estimate what the patient's dosage requirement is likely to be. Two of the more important factors influencing dosage requirements are genetic issues and the nature, severity, and chronicity of the patient's illness. Plasma level studies in identical and nonidentical twins and in first-degree blood relatives have revealed that when identical twins are given the same dose of a psychoactive compound by the same route of administration, they absorb, biotransform, and metabolize the drug in an almost identical fashion. Nonidentical twins also absorb, biotransform, and metabolize psychoactive drugs quite similarly but not as closely as in the case of identical twins. Plasma level studies have shown that first-degree blood relatives also have plasma levels within a particular range, whereas nonrelated individuals may have a twenty- to forty-fold difference between the high and the low plasma level produced by the same dosage of a psychoactive drug given by the same route of administration. For these reasons, obtaining a family drug history may provide valuable clues about what a patient's dosage requirement may be, independent of the nature, severity, and chronicity of his illness.

The nature of the patient's illness may make him a candidate for a particular psychoactive drug, but the safe and effective dosage of the drug will depend on the severity and duration of the illness. Lithium, for example, may be the drug of choice for mania but it must be acknowledged that the more severe the mania, the greater will be the degree of the patient's disturbed pathophysiology. This fact influences markedly how the patient's body will handle lithium. Thus, severe manics require and tolerate initial high doses of lithium, whereas the milder the mania the less lithium is required. If physicians do not pay attention to the severity of illness, they may overdose with lithium and produce lithium intoxication, or underdose and fail to achieve symptom control.

Besides making a specific clinical diagnosis and estimating the severity of the disorder, a physician also should attempt to ascertain the duration of the illness. Neuroleptics represent good therapy for schizophrenia, but they are most effective when administered in the early stages of schizophrenia and their effectiveness diminishes the longer the schizophrenia has existed before neuroleptic therapy is instituted. Thus, acute schizophrenic patients respond quickly to low doses of neuroleptics, but the more chronic the schizophrenia (and thus the more metabolically different the patient is compared to early schizophrenia) the higher the dosage of the neuroleptic must be and the more treatment resistant the patient is likely to be.

The influence of duration of illness on dosage requirements and therapeutic response is illustrated also by a manic depressive patient in a depressive attack. In the early stages of the illness when the patient is headed toward but has not reached the nadir of his depression, therapeutic response to even high doses of a tricyclic antidepressant is usually quite slow. But if tricyclic antidepressant therapy is started after the patient has passed the nadir of the depressive episode and is on the way back to his normal affective state, then low doses of the tricyclic often produce a rapid therapeutic response.

Twenty years of worldwide clinical experience has verified that psychopharmaceuticals when prescribed rationally can be effective, safe, and economical therapy for millions of patients. This experience also has substantiated the fact that these potent substances can also have severe maleffects. The art of using these drugs optimally and safely requires careful planning before psychopharmacotherapy is initiated, and a keen awareness of the crucial importance of making a precise, total clinical diagnosis and the difference this diagnosis makes in the final therapeutic outcome. Psychopharmacotherapy can and should make each of us better physicians and psychiatrists.

PSYCHIATRIC DIAGNOSIS AND THE LAW

HERBERT C. MODLIN, M.D.*

A conference undertaking scrutiny in depth of diagnosis promptly encounters definitional, classificatory, semantic, and conceptual dilemmas, particularly if the focus is on psychiatric diagnosis. Besides its usage as a strictly medical term, applications of diagnosis ramify to the extent that one dictionary defines it as "An investigation or analysis of the cause or nature of a condition, situation or problem" —by implication almost any condition, situation, or problem. It is commonplace to hear welfare specialists, sociological investigators, management consultants, urban planners, and political analysts speak of diagnosing a family, neighborhood, agency, industry, city, or culture.

Even in the relatively circumscribed field of general medicine diagnosis has multiple meanings. It may refer to (1) a symptom, e.g., headache of unknown etiology; (2) a syndrome of unknown cause and, therefore, uncertain treatment, e.g., psoriasis or narcolepsy; (3) a clearly understood pathological process of unknown etiology such as arthritis or multiple sclerosis; or (4) a disease of known etiology, pathology, treatment, and prognosis such as pellagra or pneumococcal lobar pneumonia.

In psychiatry the issues of diagnosis are compounded because we work with a whole person who is constantly interacting with a complex and changing environment. Many unresolved intrasystem

---

* Professor of Community and Forensic Psychiatry, The Menninger Foundation, Topeka, Kansas; Associate Clinical Professor of Psychiatry, University of Kansas Medical School, Kansas City, Kansas.

problems in our field stimulate lively debates regarding the place and value of nosological labels, classification schemes, communicative language, contextual frames of reference, and conceptual models.

1. *Diagnosis is a nosological label.* Many psychiatric clinicians are irritated about being pressed to practice the reductionism of tagging each patient's disorder with a name from the *Diagnostic and Statistical Manual* (American Psychiatric Association 1968). The listed labels appear bureaucratically built Procrustean beds into which they are expected to fit the whole range of human impairment. On the day it was published, DSM-II was partly disapproved by the very APA task force that produced it. DSM-III is in gestation and the parent APA committee anticipates that many will be unhappy with the new offspring (Task Force on Nomenclature and Statistics 1975). Nevertheless, the committee has strongly reaffirmed the importance and necessity of nosology regardless of taxonomic imperfections.

Classification is a basic methodology of science and, in medicine, of particular value in analyzing mortality, morbidity, and the results of treatment. Without classification we cannot learn of certain things we must know. Nosology facilitates communication. Exchange of knowledge among scientists is of particular importance in the mental health field in that we have so much yet to discover about those afflictions of mankind commonly called mental illnesses. The burgeoning use of computers necessitates an internationally certified set of communicable symbols adapted to the computers' as yet primitive vocabulary of names and numbers. Uniformity in diagnosis is essential for compendious communication with governmental, insurance, and other recently inaugurated regulatory agencies such as utilization review committees and professional standards review organizations. With the advent of national health insurance, medical nosology will verily be cast in concrete.

2. *Diagnosis is an explanation.* As a psychiatric resident I was fortunate to work under a chief who forbade the use of diagnostic labels in referring to or writing about a patient. He required that

the diagnosis at the end of each case report be one or more descriptive paragraphs. When the case was closed, a diagnostic label was selected to appease the medical records librarian. Emphasis on diagnostic understanding has been for years articulately propounded in the writings of Karl Menninger. In his *Manual* (1962) he wrote: "The psychiatric diagnosis, then, is not the ascription of a name to a group of symptoms but a complex set of conclusions: descriptive, analytic and evaluative. It describes an environment and an individual and their interaction, with particular reference to an unsatisfactory kind of interaction which has developed and which is seen in the patient in a certain form. A psychiatric diagnosis is always polydimensional, multidisciplinary and continuous" (p. 92).

3. *Diagnosis is a point of view.* Part of our uneasiness about mental illness stems from our varied concepts of causality. The obscurity of etiology in mental illness vivifies several unverified hypotheses, such as organic, neurochemical, psychodynamic, behavioral, interactional, and social explanations for our patients' deviations from theoretically constructed norms. In America, neurosis appears to epitomize mental illness, influenced as it is by psychoanalytic concepts; and we are inclined to view with alarm symptoms of a character too severe or regressed to fit our consensual impressions of neurosis. Since we seem to prize cognitive sanity, any phenomenon we can label "thought disorder" prompts us to search through the lists of psychoses. A broad cultural value system may be involved here as American psychiatrists, compared to fellow practitioners in the United Kingdom, tend to overdiagnose schizophrenia and organic brain syndrome (Cooper *et al.* 1972; Ducksworth & Ross 1975).

In assessing these several possible variations of diagnosis, we must confront the issue of models, particularly with respect to the pertinence of the medical model of disease in the mental health field. Extremists declare that the medical model is outmoded, even detrimental to the work of the mental health professions; others hold that it is the one model on which we can validly base our claim that we gather data and evaluate results scientifically. Siegler and

Osmund (1974) analyzed the professional work of numerous medical and nonmedical mental health colleagues and observed eight different conceptual models in actual use: the moral model, impaired model, psychoanalytic model, social model, psychedelic model, conspiratorial model, family interaction model, and medical model. They might have added one more, the public health model.

Even with the best possible nosological scheme, adherence to one model of procedure, consensually validated definitions, and traditional psychodynamic formulations, we are in trouble. One summary statement of our diagnostic competence reads as follows: ". . . psychiatric diagnosis is complex and beset by confusing conceptual difficulties as well as by firmly rooted attitudes and affects that contribute a degree of irrationality to virtually all of the currently popular positions" (Fitzgibbons & Hokanson 1973, p. 972). It has been shown that validity and reliability of diagnosis can be questioned; that diagnostic concepts vary significantly with a diagnostician's professional identity, theoretical orientation, and the type of organization in which he practices; that diagnosticians jointly conducting a psychiatric interview disagree on what they observe, what they infer, and how they employ nosology.

I need not labor our problems further. The point in this abbreviated analysis of our intrasystem diagnostic difficulties is that in an intersystem excursion, such as collaborating with the legal system, this confusion is the kind of baggage we carry with us. It is little wonder that our legal colleagues are confused and sometimes impatient with our inexact, wordy, and contradictory explanations about our evaluation of a given person's mental condition. We are told that we are unintelligible, that our data are complicated and imprecise, that our conclusions are often tenuous and vague, and that our prognoses are unreliable. Granting that our diagnostic formulations may serve us in planning treatment, we are informed they do not serve forensic purposes (Slovenko 1973).

The medical model of disease is fully accepted and firmly entrenched in the law. The great majority of doctors consulted by trial attorneys and testifying in court are nonpsychiatric physicians. It has been estimated that (if we disregard divorce actions) seventy percent of all the cases on all the dockets of all American trial courts are personal injury suits. In all those suits medical testimony is required to substantiate injury or disease and resultant impairment or disability. Thus, trial attorneys become familiar with how physicians collect data, pursue differential diagnosis, and arrive at diagnostic, therapeutic, and prognostic conclusions within the framework of the medical model. They expect comparable procedures from medical practitioners in psychiatry.

Recently, in testifying before a workmen's compensation commissioner, I described in some detail a claimant's premorbid personality development, the psychological impact of the highway crash, the unsatisfactory post-accident medical management, the influence on his disability of a worsening marital relationship, and his adverse reaction to two years of unemployment. When I finished my exposition, the commissioner patiently asked, "Yes, Doctor, but does the patient have a traumatic neurosis?" I had squandered half an hour of his time and mine. All he wanted or could use from me was a legally relevant diagnosis, an activating signal of communication. He could then proceed to dispose of the case. The medical model is implemental in the practice of law.

A primary reason a psychiatrist appears in the legal arena is because he has diagnosed mental illness in a litigant. Occasionally the psychiatrist's testimony may be useful when he has made a determination that a litigant is *not* mentally ill. The testifying psychiatrist is given the legally defined role of expert witness which means that he has been accepted as having more knowledge pertinent to the case than the average man. He is there to supplement the jury's common knowledge and is, in a sense, an expert consultant to the jury and/or judge. His recognized expertise is in the area of mental illness and, in contrast to the clinical psychologist, psychiatric social worker, or psychiatric nurse, who may also at times be expert witnesses, he is called always as an expert *medical* witness who practices a medical specialty. He is presumed to have skill in diagnosis, treatment, and prognosis, but it is his ability as a diagnostician that is crucial in many legal decisions.

In personal injury suits and workmen's compensation claims, disability caused by mental illness must be proved or the plaintiff has no case. In lawsuits impugning a citizen's mental competence to execute a will, deed, or contract, it must be shown that the citizen was mentally ill at the time he signed the document or there may be no legal case. In trials involving the criminal law, competency to stand trial is frequently an issue; the question being, "Is the accused, *by reason of mental illness or defect,* incompetent to stand trial?" If, in the course of preparation for trial, the defendant's capability to be responsible for his criminal actions is doubtful, then the question becomes, "Did the accused at the time of committing the offense, *by reason of mental illness or defect,* inherently lack capacity to know what he was doing and to conform his conduct to the requirements of the law?"

A second intersystem problem is that, although "by reason of mental illness" is the factor requiring a psychiatrist's participation in the legal process, the diagnostic search may stop there. Once the actuality of mental illness has been attested, the kind of illness is less significant than its effects. The issues to be decided in court are legal, not medical.

In a suit to break or set aside a will, if the probability of mental illness in the testator has been established, the inquiry shifts to the matter of impairment narrowly conceived: "Was the testator aware that he was signing his will?"; "Could he appraise the quality and quantity of his property?"; "Did he understand who were his legal heirs?" Whether his impairment was rooted in schizophrenia, presenile dementia, or brain tumor is not especially relevant to settlement of the legal dispute.

It may be of vital importance to the psychiatrist in concluding his diagnostic evaluation (and, incidentally, to his patient) whether the final label he ascribes to the patient is *psychotic depressive reaction* or *manic depressive psychosis.* The implications for treatment and the nature of the prognosis may depend appreciably upon which diagnosis is best substantiated by the clinical findings. In court these diagnostic niceties may be immaterial: The psychiatrist is queried concerning the litigant's mental capacity and probable intent on the day he signed away his property, agreed to marry the woman, shot his neighbor's dog, or refused to pay his income tax. Similarly, in the criminal law, an attorney in pursuing the so-called insanity defense needs to elicit from an expert psychiatric witness data to sustain his adversary position, not the psychiatrist's therapeutic position. The attorney needs evidence, if it exists, that his client did not fully comprehend the illegality of his behavior and/ or could not control it. Here again, whether the impairment resulted from paranoid schizophrenia or a paranoid state or a toxic psychosis or a subdural hematoma may be of only secondary importance.

A third intersystem obstacle is that diagnoses serve dissimilar objectives in psychiatry and the law (Matthews 1970). In our daily practice, understanding a patient's difficulties prefaces a therapeutic plan of action for relieving discomfort and/or disability. Unless the diagnostic process facilitates treatment it is of little worth. One of the standard criticisms of impersonal nosology is that it emphasizes patients' similarities rather than their differences; another criticism is that it refers to diseases rather than to the individuals afflicted. In law, the outcome of a diagnosis can be acquittal, exemption, or vindication. A litigant, if judged sufficiently ill, will not be held to such stringent social and moral standards of behavior as a healthy person (Moore 1975).

A fourth example of intersystem problems is exemplified by the familiar battle of the experts, the seemingly wide disagreement on diagnosis of two or more psychiatrists in court. At first glance this issue may seem an intrasystem problem and, to some extent, it is; but it comes to full flower most dramatically through tender cultivation in the legal garden.

Following the medical model, the examining and cross-examining attorneys in their zeal to ascertain the presence or absence of disease often ask for a nosological label, and vest the testimony of the expert witness with authoritative credibility and persuasiveness. After all, the jury members have some knowledge of how doctors work, and the attorney may wish to emphasize that this expert on the witness stand with his unfamiliar vocabulary and wordy explanations is, nevertheless, a legitimate doctor. Thus the battle may be joined and the record cluttered with learned and/or heated disputation regarding paranoid schizophrenia versus schizoid personality versus sociopathic personality with psychotic episodes. Confusion rather than clarification is the predictable result. The psychiatrist resolves not to get caught in such a hassle again.

Some of the psychiatric-legal problems, dilemmas, and conflicts I have described all too briefly can be tempered, even resolved;

they are not inevitable. A psychiatrist can contribute positively to working relationships with the law in several ways:

First, the psychiatrist must be thoroughly prepared to testify in court. But he should practice his profession for the patient's benefit, giving no thought to compromises or deviations connected with legal tasks he may eventually be asked to participate in. In diagnostic work with a patient who has a legal as well as a mental problem, he should not depart from his best clinical effort. Only when he has made a diagnostic formulation to his satisfaction, within his own conceptual framework and vocabulary, should he then decide what parts of his data concerning the patient he may responsibly offer to legalists and how he can best convey it to them. If his evaluation has been solidly prepared, his courtroom experience should not be traumatic. He can then explain in detail the basis for his expert opinion; he will be prepared to parry the thrusts of an astute cross-examiner. He will be prepared also to refute, even to make superfluous, an accusation that in court he clings to conclusory labels without explaining the origin, development, or manifestations of a disease in terms enlightening to a jury. To lay critics of psychiatrists those labels often seem designed so as not to betray the incognizance of and irrelevance to the case being tried of the psychiatric expert's testimony (Bazelon 1974).

Second, the psychiatric participant in a legal process needs a working concept of social systems theory, a full awareness that in court he is a visitor in a nonmedical system concerned with nonmedical decisions involving nonpatients (Modlin 1972). The principal in the trial may have been his patient, but in court he becomes a litigant, plaintiff, or defendant seeking a solution to his legal problem, not his medical problem. Psychiatrists should not expect the legal game to be played by medical rules.

Third, the psychiatrist's real function in court is as a consultant or educator, not just a witness. Since I have learned in practicing community psychiatry to perform the role of mental health consultant to the welfare system and the industrial system, I experience measurably greater poise in the legal system. Trying to understand

and respond to the legal as well as the medical issues, I have accepted the responsibility to assist the legal system, however I can, to practice better law.

Fourth, the psychiatrist should be prepared to function within the medical model as it is understood by lawyers. The courtroom is not the place to convert the attorneys, jury, and judge to a conceptual model conceivably more dear to the psychiatrist. If we are not willing and ready to say the subject person is sick, how he is sick, and to what extent he is sick, our communication with our interrogators is less than adequate.

Fifth, the psychiatrist must avoid becoming caught up in the nosological debate. When I am asked by an attorney for my diagnosis, I usually counter with a request for his definition of diagnosis: Does he want a diagnostic label or a statement of diagnostic understanding concerning what is wrong with the litigant? This simple maneuver often can forestall the battle of the experts. Psychiatrists may disagree on the preferred diagnostic label, but they frequently agree that the accused is ill or ineffective or disturbed. They may disagree on the legal, philosophical, or moral issues, but they are likely to concur regarding what is wrong with the patient (Halleck 1969). These matters can be discussed in a pretrial conference with an attorney, and he can be given suggestions about interrogating both his own expert witness and the opposing psychiatrist so as to emphasize the litigant's condition rather than nosological and ideological biases of the expert witnesses.

It is probable that not only scientific but also moral, ethical, and political standards influence definitions of mental illness. Surely our cultural value systems are involved and, since they change with time, they affect the behavior of both our patients and ourselves (Salzman 1973). The manifestations of psychiatric syndromes change over the decades both qualitatively and quantitatively; and diagnostic methods, too, mirror new knowledge, more sophisticated perceptions, and refined techniques and tools. It is a wise and responsible psychiatrist who feels humble when rendering what others may hope will be a definitive diagnostic statement. We should bolster ourselves, however, with the thought that fallible though our efforts may be at times, psychiatrists probably understand better than anyone else why people behave as they do. Their insights can be of service in that the law, too, is vitally concerned with deviant behavior, with motivation and intent, and with determination of responsibility for personal conduct. Both psychiatrists and lawyers influence social decisions; they need all the help they can afford each other.

References

AMERICAN PSYCHIATRIC ASSOCIATION: *Diagnostic and Statistical Manual of Mental Disorders*, Ed. 2. Washington, DC: Author, 1968.
BAZELON, D. L.: The Perils of Wizardry. *Am. J. Psychiatry* 131(12):1317–22, 1974.
COOPER, J. E. et al.: *Psychiatric Diagnosis in New York and London*. London: Oxford University Press, 1972.
DUCKSWORTH, G. S. & ROSS, H.: Diagnostic Differences in Psychogeriatric Patients in Toronto, New York and London, England. *Can. Med. Assoc. J.* 112:847–51, 1975.
FITZGIBBONS, DAVID & HOKANSON, DEAN: The Diagnostic Decision-Making Process: Factors Influencing Diagnosis and Changes in Diagnosis. *Am. J. Psychiatry* 130(9):972–75, 1973.
HALLECK, SEYMOUR: A Critique of Current Psychiatric Roles in the Legal Process. In *Law and the Behavioral Sciences*, Lawrence Friedman & Stewart Macaulay, eds. New York: Bobbs-Merrill, 1969.
MATTHEWS, ARTHUR, JR.: *Mental Disability and the Criminal Law*. Chicago: American Bar Foundation, 1970.
MENNINGER, KARL: *A Manual for Psychiatric Case Study*. New York: Grune & Stratton, 1962.
MODLIN, H. C.: The Physician and the Legal System. *JAMA* 221(12):1387–89, 1972.
MOORE, M. S.: Mental Illness and Responsibility. *Bull. Menninger Clin.* 39(4): 308–23, 1975.
SALZMAN, LEON: Changing Styles in Psychiatric Syndromes: Historical Overview. *Am. J. Psychiatry* 130(2):147–49, 1973.
SIEGLER, MIRIAM & OSMUND, HUMPHRY: *Models of Madness, Models of Medicine*. New York: Macmillan, 1974.
SLOVENKO, RALPH: *Psychiatry and Law*. Boston: Little, Brown, 1973.
TASK FORCE ON NOMENCLATURE AND STATISTICS: Progress Report on the Development of DSM-III. Panel presentation, 128th Annual Meeting, American Psychiatric Association, Anaheim, California, May 7, 1975.

OBJECTIONS TO DIAGNOSIS AND DIAGNOSTIC PSYCHOLOGICAL TESTING DIAGNOSED

STEPHEN A. APPELBAUM, Ph.D.*

Here are some frequently heard objections to diagnosis, whether it is done through psychiatric interviewing, other clinical observation, or psychological testing. These objections apply most pointedly to psychological testing, however, since diagnosis is at the heart of the testing enterprise.

1. *Diagnosing people is a hyperabstract, cognitive, intellectual exercise associated with a loss of feeling toward and emotional contact with a patient.* This objection reflects the hoary, but still burning dialectic which runs through all clinical psychiatry and psychology: the polarization of intellect versus feeling. The human potential people, for example, accuse psychoanalysts of being mirrors, screens, and machines, while the psychoanalysts accuse human potential people of mindless emotional turn-ons. While such accusations, whether applied to therapists or testers, can be accurate, they need not be. The problem is not with diagnosis in the abstract, but how the diagnosing is done. What is called for is sufficient flexibility to alternate and blend feelings with ideas. "I see a man riding on horseback with scimitar flashing" is both a Rorschach M

---

* Senior Staff Psychologist, The Menninger Foundation; Fellow in Advanced Study, Department of Education, The Menninger Foundation; Faculty Member, Topeka Institute for Psychoanalysis, Topeka, Kansas.

response and an exciting creative production. The interpersonal diagnostic process can either be a meeting between two computers or a human interaction around a shared task.

2. *Diagnosis is inhuman in that it is something done to, or perpetrated upon another—the patient is a passive object of the diagnostician's scrutiny.* First, assuming that to some extent this statement may be true, what of it? The purpose of a clinical situation is to do the most helpful thing for the patient, and if this task involves making him temporarily the object of an investigation, that seems a small price in exchange for increasing the likelihood that he will get the most helpful treatment. This objection smacks of an insidious contamination of technical procedures with social and political values. Democracy may be a fine form of government, but it need not in every instance create the best conditions for efficiently learning facts relevant to a patient's welfare. The active-passive, authoritarian-submissive model does not, however, even fit the facts of sophisticated individual testing. In the course of such testing we offer the patient many opportunities to participate actively, in a sense authoritatively, in the process. Indeed, one of the things we are diagnosing is the patient's capacity *to* participate actively, to take initiative, and to assume responsibility for his responses.

One such example is inquiry into Rorschach responses, when we call forth a patient's capacity to account for his productions. Another is the inquiry into what a patient may think about his TAT stories. Asking why he hesitated before he gave his association to a stimulus word and what the connection was between his association and that word are further opportunities for him to participate. The patient who assumes the role of passive victim, or assumes that this role is the only model for the testing relationship, is already providing a good deal of diagnostic information about his self-esteem, about his attitude toward himself and others, and how he and others can be expected to behave toward each other. People who get exercised about psychological testing on the grounds that it is antidemocratic may be telling us much the same things about themselves.

3. *Diagnosis leads simply to putting people into pigeonholes, and labeling them. Furthermore, such labels are often used as sophisti-*

cated namecalling and have derogatory legal implications. This criticism is justified when diagnostic categories or labels are indeed used in this way. But diagnostic categories and labels reflect the fact that people fall into recognizable categories, that people in such categories show reasonably positive correlations between one and the other's various characteristics. Thus, the label or category can be helpful as a kind of shorthand, a useful piece of orienting language. As in Robert Holt's analogy, if you want to find someone in a strange city, it is helpful to know the categories—neighborhood, apartment building, and apartment. How narrow a category is required depends on the question one wishes to answer. The greater the array of treatment choices which are available for the patient, the finer the diagnostic discriminations must be.

4. *Diagnosis can be used for political purposes, for putting dissenters in jails disguised as hospitals, for finding excuses to exclude minority groups from jobs.* Such a subversion of a helping profession and a science is, of course, a grave possibility, but that concern is a political and social issue, not a technical one. Such hypocritical motives are irrelevant to the theoretical and practical status of diagnosis in a genuine *clinical* context.

5. *Diagnosis is not necessary anyway.* This point of view has two major sources. One of these goes back to when there was little treatment available, when mental illness was considered hopeless. The necessary and sufficient diagnosis under such circumstances was done by the patient himself through presenting those complaints that identified him as mentally ill. The crudity of the diagnosis matched the crudity of options stemming from it. The second antidiagnostic source stems from the beginnings of psychoanalysis. No one knew then who could profit or be hurt by it. The only way to find out was to try a standard procedure on every patient who presented himself to the analyst. Experience and study over the intervening decades have taught us that in principle there are a wide range of options, decisions, and actions which we have reason to believe may be helpful to different kinds of people with different kinds of goals in different kinds of circumstances. These include drugs, environmental changes, bodily manipulations, and individual,

group, and family therapy. They include also behavior modification, the range of therapies within the human potential movement and, within dynamic psychotherapy, the degree to which the patient requires support as against uncovering or expressive work. While it sometimes seems true that anything that one does may be helpful to some patients or useless to others, such a nihilistic position has not been substantiated. Short of that nihilism, we are faced either with guessing among the array of possibilities, or else diagnosing with a view toward matching the patients' capacities with what treatment interventions can be made available to coordinate with them.

Another order of criticism of diagnostic testing is that though diagnosing may be necessary, it can be done just as well and less expensively by clinical interview. Interview versus test is, however, a simplistic formulation. We really need answers to the question which take into consideration the differences in skills between junior and senior interviewers and testers, and differences in the kinds of information that can be tapped by interviewer and tester. Even if the recommendations to the patient should happen simply to duplicate one another, they may well be made more flexibly, confidently, and evocatively if they are based upon two opinions rather than one, and if the diagnostic understanding behind the recommendation is as rich and delineated as two differing sources of information can make it. Both diagnostic interviews and diagnostic testing are systematic ways of understanding people, and the difference between these procedures is often exaggerated. However, diagnostic testing has certain a priori advantages over the interview. Since the same stimuli are given to each patient the examiner is in a position to establish norms. An interviewer who tries to keep emotionally in touch with his patient can rarely at the same time standardize all of his questions and interventions. Further, the ambiguity of many of the test materials allows an examination of the deeper levels of personality which is more difficult to achieve during interviews. In the Psychotherapy Research Project of the Menninger Foundation, a study was made of the relative effectiveness of psychological testing compared to all other sources of psychiatric information with respect to global diagnostic understanding, treatment recommendations, and treatment predictions. Both the testing done for research purposes and the ordinary clinical test reports were better predictors for all three questions than was the psychiatric material.

The problems with diagnostic testing are less those implicated by the accusations of its critics than are those inherent nowadays in the enterprise itself. Maximizing the usefulness of diagnostic testing is a difficult and demanding task. There is no more reason to assume that any student who makes it through graduate school will become a top-flight tester than to assume that any student who makes it through medical school and wants to become a psychiatrist will become a top-flight psychotherapist, although we as members of these professions, and as a society, act as if we believe it to be so. With the best of training, not all psychologists and psychiatrists become good diagnosticians. And it was never true that all programs of clinical psychology offered high quality training in diagnostic testing. In the last fifteen years such training has become increasingly *less* available.

The testing enterprise can be viewed as a chain made of three major links: the test responses proper, a theory with which to integrate and conceptualize these responses, and knowledge of what to do on the basis of this information.* If any link in the chain is broken, the enterprise collapses. Training and experience have to be made available to achieve expertise in *all three* of these areas of knowledge and practice.

Testing is expensive of time and money. The quality of the work has to be commensurate, and the clinical context in which it takes place has to be able to make sufficient use of diagnostic testing in order to justify the expense. Unless these conditions are met, the critics of psychological testing are correct when they say that it is simply not worth what it costs.

Finally, the test report remains one of the most difficult pieces of prose ever devised or required. Too often testers have arbitrarily simplified reports into a collection of mostly first-order observa-

---

* The last point stems from the classical rule in prediction that one must know the situation to which he is predicting. And yet, for example, we have testers confidently predicting success or failure in psychoanalysis even though they have neither experienced nor practiced psychoanalysis themselves.

tions, even test scores, or gone to the opposite extreme of extrapolating test findings into highly abstract, metapsychological (and usually unreadable) formulations. Instead, test reports should be written not as reports at all in the laboratory sense, but as guides to practical action. They should be cast implicitly in the terms of an overall clinical theory, with occasional movements toward test observations on the one hand and somewhat higher order abstraction on the other. Practically every statement in the report should be answerable to the question of what difference it makes to the patient to have this statement included.

One goal of those psychologists who feel strongly about the usefulness of diagnostic testing is political. We hope to call attention to, and generate discussion of, the lessened influence, practice, and training in diagnostic testing in recent years, to examine the reasons for this decline, and to suggest that science, education, and clinical practice are the worse for it. We do so in the hope that such renewed consciousness and discussion will influence universities, clinicians, professors, and students to deploy power, within themselves and upon others, in order to make facilities for training and administrative arrangements for practice consonant with the increased use of diagnostic tests. Yet we should realize that no amount of argument and political pressure will, or should, reinvigorate the testing enterprise, without simultaneous attempts at solving such problems as I have suggested lie within the enterprise itself. Testing, and diagnosis in general, should not be taken on faith, any more than treatment should. If its proponents claim more than they can deliver, they may gain in the short run but only postpone their ultimate failure. We ought not influence people to buy potentialities alone. Our task is to demonstrate proficiency and effectiveness, to build rather than to inflate. Our first adversaries should be ourselves.

PSYCHOLOGICAL TESTING AND THE MIND OF THE TESTER

SYDNEY SMITH, Ph.D.*

Psychiatry and clinical psychology share a unique affliction. They are the only branches of the human sciences where the value of diagnosis is a matter of dispute. A diagnostic statement in psychiatry is likely to be clouded by differences in theoretical persuasion, contradictions stemming from terminological fads, confusions over the usefulness of idiosyncratic diagnostic systems (like Kelly's personal construct theory or the language of Daseinanalysis), or disagreements about definitions of even the most basic terms. *Schizophrenia*, for example, or the term *borderline state* have almost as many definitions as there are writers about these conditions. Generally a medical diagnosis is more straightforward, more likely to be based on laboratory observations, and more likely to result in a specific treatment prescription whose course or outcome can be predicted with a fair degree of accuracy. In contrast, the psychiatrist is likely to use the same treatment on his patients regardless of the diagnosis. Whether the patient is suffering from depression or schizophrenia or a form of character disorder, he will most likely be treated with phenothiazines.

The fact that such difficulties exist in diagnosis has not characteristically served as a spur to resolving these conundrums, but

---

* Chief Clinical Psychologist, and Director, Postdoctoral Training Program in Clinical Psychology, The Menninger Foundation, Topeka, Kansas. Editor, *Bulletin of the Menninger Clinic*.

have more often been seized upon as a rationale for the notion that
diagnosis does not much matter. In many psychiatric settings, the
practice of continuing to assign a diagnosis to a patient is done
more out of habit or because of institutional requirements than
out of any conviction of its usefulness. Of course, if the treater
has only one therapeutic arrow in his quiver, then diagnosis loses
its meaning, at least in the sense of differentiating one disorder from
another in a way that allows a choice of appropriate treatment. If
all one has to offer, for example, is a form of behavior modification
or electric convulsive therapy, then diagnosis is mistakenly deni-
grated as having no value, thus missing the importance of distinguishing this patient's complaints from every other patient's complaints. But if the treater is sensitive to the role of conflict, to the
existing varieties of ego states, to the conditions of adaptive strength
or weakness, to the range of human defenses and resistances and
to their pathological implications, then the treater will appreciate
the fact that all this information may point up the wisdom of
choosing one treatment modality over another.

But this argument is a global one; indeed, these broader issues
of deciding whether a patient would most benefit from supportive
psychotherapy or psychoanalysis, from marital counseling or hospitalization, from individual or group treatment, can often be satis-
factorily decided without the help of psychological tests. Or if
the evaluator is interested only in describing the hysterical person
or the obsessional character, then one is dealing with concepts
so overdetermined as not to be useful in a specific clinical instance.
But the psychological tester deals with real cases, with individual
patients, not with the generalized person. Or at least the hope is
that the final report on the test results will reveal the uniqueness
of the particular patient, portraying those life paradigms that describe only that individual's psyche.

A case could be made for saying that bringing all the test references on a single patient together in all their uniqueness into a
test report is a manifestation of poetic expressiveness. I am not
speaking of rhapsodical writing. I am talking about lean, disci-
plined prose with a minimum of objectives and a commitment to
brevity. The test report should have an evocative power because
it is written for someone who will work therapeutically with the

patient or someone who may have to make a subtle treatment disposition. The kind of empathic participation the examiner takes in the patient's test responses can stir the reader of the report to an understanding of the same nuances. A careful amassing of evidence from the tests or a sparingly picked sample response can convey with vivid poignancy the nature of the patient's inner world. This task is an essential part of the clinical situation, and we ought not to settle for a dry, mechanical analysis which might be diagnostically correct but does nothing to make the patient come to life. Here are two examples taken from two different test reports on two different patients but ostensibly describing the same diagnostic condition:

Example 1: The patient could be described as an infantile personality, overlaid by narcissistic, masochistic, and hysterical features. Her infantile core is reflected by her pervasive immersion in affect-laden, wish-fulfilling fantasy, her predominant concern with receiving nurturant supplies in relationships with others, and her minimal tolerance for anxiety and depression. Her narcissistic features are manifested by arbitrariness, self-indulgent protection against harsh judgments, denial of inadequacy, subtle projection, and devaluation of others. Her external reality can become highly permeable and her thoughts drive-dominated. She defends against disorganization by undoing, rationalization, projection, repression, and detachment.

Example 2: With deadening consistency, the tests roll up a mountain of evidence supporting a diagnosis of an infantile, narcissistic character structure. With her every utterance, one gets caught up in a tidal wave of egocentricity, tangential thinking, infantile demandingness, and a facetious flippancy that carries the examination procedure further and further away from its objective until it finally is cast on the barren rocks of her emptiness, her unreflectiveness, and her remarkable incapacity to develop even rudimentary ties to other people. She has developed sufficient alertness and mimicry to pick up the standard clichés about "feelings" and "love" and "guilt." But invariably probing inquiry reveals only great hollows in her psychological development. With this patient, test inquiry is much like exploring an empty cave, where one becomes chilled from the absence of light and warmth, hearing only the echo of one's own probe tapping against the walls.

What one senses in these excerpts, brief as they are, is that the second writer, unlike the first one, was living out the responses of the patient in his own mind, had taken the patient for a brief moment as an object within himself so that the psychological knowledge the tester has of his patient becomes an inner experience. This conception means that the tester's understanding of the processes within the patient come about through a re-creation of those processes within himself.

Recently the historian Peter Loewenberg (1976) wrote a paper containing a remarkable paragraph describing the work of Wilhelm Dilthey, the German philosopher of history. Writing in the early part of this century, Dilthey articulated the task of the historian as: ". . . an inner reliving of the development of individuation . . . .[and] On the basis of this, [the] placing of oneself in the situation; [and in] this transposition, the highest form in which the totality of mental life can be effective in understanding, arises— imitation or identification." Loewenberg tells us that "Dilthey was the earliest conceptualizer of the use of sympathy and empathy as tools of cognition in historical research."

It seems to me Dilthey is saying something as a professional historian I am trying to convey as a professional psychologist: That a patient's feeling when it is lived empathically by the tester may be a pathway from the manifest to the latent content of the patient's response and thus also a way of reconstructing the past.

Freud wanted to show how the latent thought is derived from the manifest content. In a real sense the psychological tester has the same task in making inferences from his data. The way a person turns latent content into manifest thought speaks to the total structure of the personality. From the test responses it is often possible to reconstruct this process, a task probably more important than trying to trace the history of the latent thought. Actually it is the working through of the process of getting from the latent to the manifest content that leads to cure. That task is not the psychodiagnostician's, but it does lead to the realization that in one sense an analysis is nothing but a complete diagnosis. Reconstruction, then, is not merely a matter of reconstructing the past but of reconstructing the process that led to the present state in which the patient finds himself. Even the job of analysis is something more than digging up the past. Freud himself was more a process-thinker than an archeologist. It is also true that as one reconstructs the process, one also discovers the past. This function is not unique to psychology; every science has engaged in it. What is unique in psychodiagnostics, as in psychoanalysis, is the nature of the subject matter for such discovery.

We can approach this task in part through an analysis of the patient's verbalizations. I am referring to the patient's style of thought, outlook on life, his subjective experiences of thinking and feeling. These data always occupy an important place in understanding the patient. They represent formal aspects of the test even though we have no scores for them. They are not "test content" because such things as a patient's style of thought cut across all the tests and run through every patient's verbalizations. And the inferences one draws from these data can extend in all directions—dynamic, genetic, adaptive. There is no one facet of the personality to which analysis of verbalization is restricted. Again, this task represents a poetic aspect of test analysis, and it will probably always remain poetic.

There are three major obstacles to accomplishing the task we have set out for psychological testing—the patient, the tester, and the tests themselves. As psychologists we have to be concerned about the adequacy of our instruments: Are they going to tell us what we think they will and will they tell us reliably? But probably these questions represent the least of our troubles because almost any task can serve as the proving ground for the projective hypothesis. Dr. Herbert Schlesinger used to demonstrate to classes of wide-eyed neophyte clinicians how he could turn the chance contents of his pockets into a respectable sorting test. The tests we use with regularity, of course, do have certain advantages. For one thing they have been developed with an eye toward standardization which allows for the development of established norms. The patient's functioning can in this way be systematically observed; and the psychologist, on the basis of repeated experience with the same tests under the same testing conditions, develops his own internalized norms. The idea that this sensitive job can be relegated to a technician is based on the idea that the tests can yield nothing but a mechanical result. But the good psychotherapist who wants the help of test findings knows that it takes another highly skilled and experienced psychotherapist-tester to recognize what a treater needs to know about his patient.

The patient may also be an obstacle to the diagnostic task in testing, not because he may resist the process—his resistances in testing as in treatment are grist for the mill—but because his illness or his symptomatology may not be accessible for study. We are all aware of the fact that with some patients we can establish the presence of thought disorder within a short period of testing, whereas with other patients to arrive at the same finding may take considerably more time, and even then the result may remain a matter of dispute among experienced testers. This difficulty may be related to the nature of the pathology. As Kendell (1975) points out in his short monograph on diagnosis, there are consistent differences in the reliability with which a diagnosis may be secured. In general the psychoses can be established with greater reliability than the neuroses, the organic psychoses with greater reliability than the functional psychoses, and so on. When the illness possesses features specific to itself—as in anorexia nervosa—the diagnosis is easy, but if no such features characterize the illness, the job becomes more difficult.

Of course the psychological tester is not so much concerned with diagnostic issues as broad as those I have just described, but it is true that in multifaceted symptom pictures, the answers to diagnostic questions may be more ambiguous.

But the most serious obstacle to the task of diagnostic testing is the examiner himself. Schafer (1954) has explicated this point so well I do not need to dwell on it. The psychologist is his own primary instrument of research. He is not only the collector but the perceiver and interpreter of his data. In subtle ways, this process can go awry. For some psychologists, testing represents an assault on the patient. On some level of awareness, the psychologist may look upon test inquiry as a lethal weapon, not to be used in probing the patient because it may do great damage. (These same magical notions may exist in the psychiatrist, making him reluctant to refer patients for testing.) To what extent this attitude represents a reaction formation in the examiner, masking his wish to do the patient damage, or to what extent the examiner's reluctance to inquire into the patient's test responses is an effort to defend himself against an expected arousal of hostility or aggression in the patient would have to be determined in the individual case. Or there are those further instances in which the tester refuses to see pathology but attempts to explain away the patient's every quirk on cultural or sociological grounds. This approach is a way of neutralizing the test findings and always represents an abandonment of the intrapsychic.

There are also those puzzling instances when good diagnosticians who are also psychotherapists feel that in taking on a new therapy case the test results would contaminate their own thinking about the patient. To avoid any influence from the test data they would rather forego—at least for a time—any study of what the tests might contribute to an illumination of the patient's pathology. At this stage of the professional development of psychological tests this attitude is as outrageous as would be a modern traveler who in venturing forth on a long and complicated journey refused to look at a roadmap because it might influence his personal choice of direction.

What I have recounted in this brief communication about testing are some evidences of its value, the need for professionalism in its application, and some of the pitfalls in the way of its proper pursuit. Even when the psychodiagnostician may be committed to psychological testing and to the diagnostic process—even when he is convinced intellectually of its soundness and its vitality—we have to remember that, just as in the process of psychotherapy or psychoanalysis, psychological testing brings the examiner into close range with the patient's pathology. It is not surprising, then, that all the pitfalls to be found in transference and countertransference phenomena apply with equal force to the testing experience. We are not dealing merely with a psychometric process carried out by a technician on a neutral object of observation, as suggested in the early literature on testing, but a relationship between the tester and

his patient which in its very complexity encompasses all that we
know about the nature of the human condition.

References

KENDELL, R. E.: *The Role of Diagnosis in Psychiatry.* Oxford, England: Aber-
deen University Press, 1975.
LOEWENBERG, PETER: Why Psychoanalysis Needs the Social Scientist and
the Historian. *Int. J. Psychoanal.*, in press, 1976.
SCHAFER, ROY: *Psychoanalytic Interpretation in Rorschach Testing, Theory
and Application.* New York: Grune & Stratton, 1954.

TOWARD AUTONOMOUS PASTORAL DIAGNOSIS

SEWARD HILTNER, Ph.D., D.D.*

The term *autonomous* to describe pastoral diagnosis suggests that pastor, priest, and rabbi should make their diagnoses primarily on the basis of their own theological and ecclesiastical convictions and practices rather than borrowing eclectically from other helping professions. The fact is, however, that autonomy can be only relative where human beings are concerned. Western theology has never been frozen at a particular point in time, refusing to learn from available sources regarded as relevant. Its relative autonomy has come not from rejecting all outside contributions but by relating those appropriately to its central focus. It is this relative sense of autonomy that I advocate rather than a compartmentalized sense that would reject all new insight automatically if it did not come wrapped in holy polyethylene.

The idea of relative autonomy correctly suggests the problem that is currently most urgent in pastoral diagnosis. During the past generation or half century the development of dynamic psychiatry, clinical psychology, and social work has generated insights into dimensions of human life that are similar to, if not at times identical with, the areas with which pastors have been traditionally concerned. Discoveries by these disciplines have been set forth, for the most part, through a semimythological terminology composed

* Professor of Theology and Personality, Princeton Theological Seminary, Princeton, New Jersey.

175

about equally of neologisms and of traditional words defined in special senses. During this same half century, pastors have been reexamining their own ministries of pastoral care or *cura animarum* or *Seelsorge*. Properly attracted by some of the illuminating findings of the other professions, they tended to get caught in the terminologies used by those groups, and frequently have downgraded not only their own terminology but also the concern and insight available in their tradition.

The problem has come, therefore, not as an imposition on the part of outside groups upon pastors, but rather by pastors accepting not only helpful new insights but also the kind of theological and philosophical amorphousness that has necessarily characterized groups united not by their theories but by their capacity to heal and help. Too often pastors have been so struck by the discoveries, and the rather bastard language in which they have been couched, that they have adopted the whole context from which they have come, that is, what is most vulnerable, and have not attempted to rework the insights within their own framework. I will discuss this later on.

If we are to move toward an understanding of pastoral diagnosis, however, that is clearly rooted in the best of our tradition but which includes all relevant new discoveries whether made by ourselves or others, it is important that we examine some other problems of pastoral diagnosis especially in the light of our theological history.

Temporarily using a rough conception of diagnosis as appraisal, examination, or evaluation, we can say that diagnosis first appeared in Christian history in terms of new members. One was not barred by being either Jew or Gentile, male or female, citizen or otherwise. For several centuries, however, new members or catechumens went through a long period of testing and apprenticeship. If they persisted, they were in. If they did not, they ruled themselves out. And if their performance was too far from the community's expectation, the latter made a negative diagnosis.

Once in the fellowship, both individual and collective diagnoses had to be made about whether one could remain a member. During the period of official persecution many Christians publicly recanted to save their lives. After the persecutions, the decision was made to readmit such persons on the grounds that the social pressure on them had been extreme.* Unhappily, not every period in the church's history has adopted such forgiving types of diagnoses.

After Christianity became the official religion of the Roman Empire, soon followed by the steady decline of that empire, the church began to develop the diagnostic system that was codified in the so-called books of penitentials (McNeill 1951; McNeill & Gamer 1938). At first issued locally by a bishop or abbot, followed by the acceptance of these guideline volumes over wider areas, these books of laws and punishments and conditions for restoration became the diagnostic guides for many centuries. They appraised the relative seriousness of a person's offense against the community, made explicit the penance to be done and, providing the person survived the ordeals, specified the conditions of his readmission to the fellowship. During the early years from the fifth or sixth centuries, either the death penalty or harsh punishment was recommended for a wide variety of offenses. During the later Middle Ages the punishments became somewhat less extreme but were hardly mild by modern standards. It should be noted that, until the beginning of nation states, the action of the church as codified in the penitential handbooks dealt with areas that later became the prerogatives of national criminal and civil law.

In Roman Catholicism the penitential handbooks were succeeded by what came to be called *pastoral theology*. Moral theology became the codification of moral principles based on religious premises, and pastoral theology codified the individual situations. Like the penitentials, this system was behavioristic in the sense that appraisal was made in terms of the externals of the offense. Pastoral theology did make some allowance for the circumstances, knowledge, and motivation, but only as partial exceptions to the basic rules set forth by moral theology. The important fact is that pastoral diagnosis became almost wholly a matter of morality, was treated legalistically and even punitively and, as one area after another of jurisdiction was taken from the church by the states, codification of the remainder became more detailed and voluminous. Even

---

* For discussion of this and other points of relevant history see Clebsch & Jaekle (1964).

though a softening of some of the harshness has been going on for decades, it was not until Vatican II that this whole system was brought under severe criticism in Roman Catholicism. At least in principle, it now seems doomed in contemporary Catholicism. For good or ill, however, it was the prevailing Catholic system of diagnosis for centuries.

After the Reformation, Protestantism showed itself to be highly suspicious of the Catholic diagnostic system in regard to moral offenses. It was generally not repugnance against the harshness of penalties, but antipathy to a priest's or pastor's usurping God's prerogatives in making such judgments that motivated the Protestant position. Protestantism arose only when nation states were also being built, and many dimensions of moral life were handled by civil and criminal law. The refusal of Protestantism to have case books, so to speak, like those of Catholicism meant that Protestant dealing with offenders was less uniform, sometimes harsher and sometimes milder. Protestants did confront a new diagnostic dimension. If a person repented after his offense, should he be restored without punishment? In any event, how could church or pastor decide if his repentance was genuine?

Before leaving premodern churches, we should note Catholicism's traditions of the confessional and of spiritual direction. Private confession to God through a priest became obligatory for all Catholics in the thirteenth century. Even serious offenses might first be confessed there, although the confessional seal meant that punishment as well as communal disclosure were brought about in other ways. It was the confessional, however, that dealt with all anxieties, guilts, fears, and other troubles of worried persons, and uneasy consciences even if no named offenses were involved. Impersonal as the procedure was, the confessional permitted the priest to exercise some diagnostic discretion with persons.

In Catholic spiritual direction the focus was usually on matters other than morality. A person had a priest as a special guide, saw him either at regular intervals or by agreement and, along with prayer, they worked together in conversational fashion on the person's "spiritual life." Here was an incipiently different form of diagnosis, also containing the seeds of developmental insight, which could have been the precursor of modern pastoral diagnosis if it had not fallen into behavioristic ruts of its own. Like psychoanalytic societies, many of the recipients of spiritual direction were themselves priests, monks, or nuns; and, whatever may be said against the legalisms into which the system fell, it did for many provide the means to prod toward a richer and more meaningful life. Although we have little literature showing how spiritual direction was actually conducted, some materials suggest that, in the best priestly hands, such guidance went far beyond problem solving and contained acute powers of diagnosing potentials as well as problems.

So far as Protestantism can be said to have carried out anything like spiritual direction, it was largely on a group rather than an individual basis. When there were face-to-face groups, as in the class meetings of early Methodism, the results in terms of "spiritual growth" of members were often remarkable. For in such groups the "spiritual condition" of each member was given consideration by the entire company (the size of which was about what Kurt Lewin later recommended). In most of Protestantism, at least beyond the early years of new churches, such discipline and practice quickly went out of fashion. Family worship and prayers were always recommended. And the pastoral calling of Protestantism, with the minister staying in a home long enough to teach, pray with, examine, and encourage both the group and individual members must have been a powerful instrument until almost our own century.* As in Catholicism, there was of course much dealing with persons who were dying, or sick by any definition, or in trouble not of their own devising. And there were many conversations, along with meetings, designed to bring persons to the point of both verbal and heartfelt confession to God of their sinfulness so that they might receive His grace in Jesus Christ and be saved from an otherwise inevitable fate. Examination of the records of the one minister of the nineteenth century who left verbatim reports of his pastoral conversations suggests that, despite the rigidity of the intellectual system in which he operated, much diagnostic wisdom was demonstrated in his dealing with persons, including the frequent transcen-

---

* The best known treatise about pastoral calling in earlier periods of Protestant history came from a nonconformist English pastor, Richard Baxter, who published The Reformed Pastor in 1656.

dence of the categories of moral problems and offenses (Spencer 1853).

Churches and pastors, and hence pastoral diagnosis, have been inevitably affected by what has been regarded as sickness or illness in any age, and by what is excluded from that category. For several centuries before the emergence of modern medicine and psychiatry, the prevailing idea of a real illness required that it run a course, that the self have no complicity in it, and that it not involve factors of morality. Thus it took a long time before alcoholism and mental illness could be seen in any way as sicknesses, and almost as long to regard tuberculosis and syphilis as illnesses. Once a person's condition was diagnosed by a physician or the public as a real illness, then pastor and church were often in the forefront in providing help, as shown in the large part played by the church in establishing hospitals and their predecessors. But the church has only in a few prophetic instances used its pastoral diagnosis to extend the illness category beyond what was prevalent. It has often shown moral courage as in working with lepers, but seldom intellectual daring as in providing the mentally ill only with exorcism or with nothing.

From these and other historical reflections, I draw the general conclusion that pastors and churches, far from having had no experience with diagnosis, have had so many bad experiences with it that, when they move out of a legalistic framework and genuinely want to help people, the last resource they are likely to look for is diagnosis. The positive aspects of diagnosis in their history—like the catechumens, Wesley's class meetings, or Catholic spiritual direction—are no longer viable as programs, and are not regarded as having diagnostic dimensions. What appears to be historically diagnostic is the legalistic and behavioristic and moralistic background of offenses, punishments, and even cruelties.

We cannot, therefore, resurrect pastoral diagnosis without reconstructing it. The combination of important new insights with the positive elements in the Bible and tradition should make reconstruction possible. But more is required than making up a package and presenting it to the clergy. For a new pastoral diagnosis to take hold, a pastor needs to understand his feeling of revulsion at the predominantly legalistic diagnoses of the past. As with any negative embedded feeling, he can get over that not by ignoring or repressing it but by understanding how it came about.

The appropriation of diagnosis by the medical profession has been so overwhelming that it is difficult to reach beneath the medical folkways toward a deeper understanding of diagnosis itself. Let me note a few medical assumptions about diagnosis. First, diagnosis is called for only when one is sick, in trouble, having pain, or when someone with power thinks such conditions exist. Second, the most desirable diagnosis has sufficient clarity for it to be basically right from then on, even if details are changed here and there. Third, the most important fact about a diagnosis is the understanding it gives the physician. Fourth, diagnosis deals with individual persons; any reference beyond persons is metaphorical. Fifth, diagnosis points to the problem, while other terms need to be used for the resources.

I mean in no way to denigrate the diagnosing process (and I hope it *is* a process not a single event) even in medicine by suggesting that I believe the medical folkways are one-sided and therefore partly wrong. In the general sense and sometimes even in medicine, diagnosis may be relevant not only when there is illness or pain but also when there is aspirational discontent with the present situation. The clarity of a diagnostic event is hardly an indicator of its profundity if we are dealing with human beings. Important as it is for the helper, physician or otherwise, to understand a diagnosis, it may be even more important for the person to understand and accept it, and indeed to make contributions in the process of reaching it. There is no good reason why diagnosis should refer only to individuals. Groups too may have problems. And confining diagnosis only to negative factors, ignoring an understanding of potential resources, is arbitrary.

Some help in the search for a more general idea of diagnosis than medicine has provided may be found in etymology. In classical Greek, knowledge or understanding is represented by the words *logos* and *gnosis*. *Logos* implied the big idea, the generality, the comprehensive, sometimes the abstract. *Gnosis* was a more everyday word, which implied not only figuring things out including very concrete things but also a personal prehension or assimilation of something. The personal element in *gnosis* was carried to extremes by the Gnostics of the second century A.D., who claimed what we now call a kind of esoteric access to truth that disdained all tests of public verifiability. But that distortion of gnosis ought not to prevent us from seeing that even the Greeks saw a difference between understanding the big idea objectively and grasping something, in today's parlance, existentially.

When the Greek *dia*, meaning through or by way of, is connected to *logos*, we get one of today's over-used words, *dialogue*, usually with no comprehension of the dialogue in Plato's sense as probing for general ideas. As the present personalizing of dialogue ignores its Greek roots, so the current use of diagnosis ignores the uniquely personal and subject side of the Greek *gnosis*. Granted that the classical Greek tongue was complex, any conception of diagnosis that remains abstract, objective, and ignores the subject, runs in the face of its derivation. Whatever diagnosis is according to the Greek terms, it cannot be less than a process in which the aim is creative assimilation by the subject to which end all other considerations, important as they may be, are secondary. The closer the matters under consideration come to the personal center, the more important is this creative appropriation.

Many if not most psychiatric diagnoses, largely because they lack the deceptive clarity of medical diagnoses, come closer to the Greek meaning. Karl Menninger (Menninger et al. 1963) in particular deserves warm commendation for warning against diagnosis as mere labeling, for viewing illnesses or difficulties along a continuum rather than in compartments, and for including appraisal of resources along with problems in diagnosis. Important as these points are as correctives to the prevailing view of diagnosis in psychiatry, however, they do not necessarily in themselves include the person (or group) as partner (within the limits of his abilities) fully in the total and continuing process of diagnosing, and they do not necessarily see the ultimate diagnostic goal as his assimilation of all possible effective knowledge about his condition including his resources. It seems to me, however, that nothing less can finally serve as a correct and constructive understanding of diagnosis, whether in medicine, psychiatry, the ministry, or elsewhere.

The discussion may now return to the urgent contemporary problem of how to make pastoral diagnosis focus theologically even though some of the ingredients of that diagnosis may not originally have come from a theological framework. Since mentioning that issue at the beginning, I have set forth two necessary intermediary points: First, I argued that the dominant diagnostic pastoral procedures of the past have been, with some exceptions, so legalistic and behavioristic that there is almost universal repugnance to them today, and that, therefore, we cannot move effectively toward a proper use of pastoral diagnosis without helping pastors to distinguish between proper diagnosis and the basic view of pastoral diagnosis that they have inherited from their past. Second, I contended that modern medicine, and even psychiatry to a lesser extent, has held and still holds to an understanding of diagnosis that is one-sided or foreshortened, either ignoring or minimizing aspects of the process that seem crucial. The implication is that a valid new pastoral diagnosis must, in addition to exploring what is uniquely pastoral, rethink the basic meaning of any diagnosis, and not permit medicine or psychiatry to dictate the definition of what is to be included in and excluded from the meaning of diagnosis.

What does it mean to assert that pastoral diagnosis should have a theological focus? What does it mean, for one important dimension, in terms of language used? It means, on the one hand, that at least some of the language used be recognizably within or traceable to the theological tradition. It does not mean of course that all the language must be traditional for that would presuppose the theological enterprise as linguistically crystallized. Relatively new concepts or translations of older concepts, however, should clearly be set within a broadly theological framework or context. If they are partly borrowed from other contexts, they should be carefully separated from those contexts.

Special language problems are posed by the emergence of modern psychodynamics stemming from Freud, and interpersonal dynamics from Freud, Lewin, and others. The insights themselves are both rich and indispensable for any helper at the human level, including the pastor. Part of the language for them is a special use of traditional terms, and part of it is new coinage, but much of it is semimythological. It is certainly eclectic. Since the insights are important, the pastor too would be depriving himself by not using them. But does he use the eclectic language, or are there adequate theological equivalents that he should employ? My answer is that sometimes one course and sometimes the other is appropriate.

At the root of virtually every dynamic discovery it is possible to find a theological intuition that has prefigured the insight.* At the same time, theology has seldom emerged with the full particularity of the insight. There may be, therefore, no specific terms in the theological vocabulary for carrying the meaning of the specific discovery even though theological language may have put its finger on the underlying point of which the particular insight is a concrete dimension. In those instances, it is proper to use the modern eclectic terms or to coin others that may seem more appropriate in a theological context.

In a book, *Pastoral Counseling*, written more than a quarter of a century ago, I suggested that dynamic insights, no matter how they are first discovered, cannot be regarded as the property of the group that finds them, but are instead a kind of village green for all professions that attempt to help human beings and enrich their lives. The language by which such insights, once found, are conveyed may be a historical accident. Perhaps theology can find a better language for its purposes. Perhaps it cannot. If circumstances suggest that the language of the group that discovered the dynamic is as good as can be found, then the pastor is not borrowing from the other group in a pejorative sense although he does well to acknowledge his sources. If all borrowing were bad, then modern psychiatry would probably be the chief offender, for its terms have been raided from mythology, literature, the exact sciences, ethics, philosophy, and even theology. Such a charge would of course be pointless.

I have spoken so far of the language used by the pastor himself in his diagnostic efforts. It is indeed his professional responsibility to see that the language he uses for clarification to himself be not inconsistent with what he represents. But what about the language he uses with the other or others? If his purpose is communication to the other, and if the other is to assimilate any insight the pastor has, thus evoking from the other whatever problem or potential

---

* Some illustrations of this point may be found in my book, *Theological Dynamics* (1972).

can aid the best diagnosis, then the pastor will clearly use no language, theological or otherwise, that impedes such a process. It is no more proper for him to insert God or faith or providence into every sentence than it would be for a psychiatrist to reiterate ego or Oedipus complex or transference.

There is, however, a subtle danger that the search for communicability in language may result in a kind of least common denominator that lacks both precision and depth. In my experience, the use of metaphor, often overtly biblical and theological, may serve as a kind of bridge language. For example, if what is being discussed is the tendency of a person to engage in behavior of which his ego-oriented conscience disapproves, the pastor may comment, "Then it is rather like the Garden of Eden situation," instead of the flat, "You feel unhappy at the discrepancy?" At times the use of metaphor may lead to discussion in explicitly theological terms, and at times it will not. The difference lies not in the desire of the pastor but in the readiness of the parishioner. It is the pastor's job, however, to open the way. If he is not at home either with theological language or with the metaphor that seems to be the bridge to it, he is probably selling short the unique contribution of his own discipline.

It should be noted that metaphor, in the sense suggested, is not just analogy in the meaning of the Greek *logos* plus *ana*, the latter suggesting a positive act; for, as was noted earlier, *logos* deals with knowledge in a general or objective sense. Charles Curran has spoken of metaphor in my sense as "anagnosis," in which the reference is personalized, individualized, and the other person taken in as a partner in the inquiry.

In the discussion above about the pastor's and the parishioner's use of language in diagnosis, I have necessarily made some reference to basic theological concepts. Most theological concepts are generalized intuitions, profoundly true and quite capable of linkage with concrete situations, but ordinarily not devised to capture nuances of the person or situation. Wherever the specifics come from that relate the intuition to the specific situation, they ought not be permitted to obscure the basic intuition.

Years of teaching pastors and theological students to do theological diagnoses of situations in which they are involved have taught me that there is a second primary temptation that pastors confront in dealing with theological concepts, namely, a tendency to view theology as an answer system rather than as a description of the way things really are at a level deeper than the obvious. When dealing with a person, for instance, who has been frequently rejected in the intimate relations of life, a pastor will at times offer as a theological diagnosis, "What he needs is the ability to love." Although the statement may be true, it offers no bridge actually to helping the person; and it is suspect also because it assumes that theology talks of an ideal to which man is to measure up, that is, theology is a kind of hortatory answer system. Similar irrelevance may be seen when a diagnostic label of *sinner* is placed on a person who has committed some antisocial acts. In such instances, I find it necessary to demonstrate that theology is a descriptive rather than a hortatory discipline, that it begins by showing how things are from its own perspective and not how they ought to be. Once the various levels of "isness" are understood, but only then, may we employ the resources from which theology stems.

It seems proper at this point to offer some illustrative situations about how pastoral diagnosis may be pursued today with relative autonomy. These examples must necessarily be brief and therefore deficient in the full flavor of the concrete process. I shall consider first two situations from mental hospitals in which I served as pastoral or theological consultant. Because of the consultant role, I was unable to follow through with the particular persons involved, that job being left to the chaplains and others. Except for that incompleteness, however, I believe I performed a proper pastoral and theological diagnostic function.

The first situation involved a man in his mid-twenties whom I will call John Brigham. During a previous period of hospitalization, brought about by an incident of erratically antisocial behavior involving only minor damage to property and none to human life, Mr. Brigham had been specially befriended by a psychiatric aide who was a member of the local Mormon church. Even during the hospitalization the general support of the aide was augmented by other church members; Mr. Brigham studied Mormon teachings; his condition improved and, upon his discharge, he joined the church group, which helped him to find a job, a place to live, and a supporting community. For some months his behavior was exemplary. Then came another antisocial incident, milder than the first, but sufficient to cause his hospital readmission. It seemed clear to the staff that Mr. Brigham was likely to have a certain amount of continuing personal instability. But he had after all got along reasonably well for more than twenty years; and, following his discharge, had done well for several months. What chances were there that interaction between him and his adopted church community could either keep his instability under control or his eruptions mild and not socially damaging?

My first act in the consultation was to inquire what kind of Mormon group was involved. The question itself was a surprise to the staff group, who had assumed that all Mormons had Salt Lake City as headquarters. Since there were no Mormons in the staff group, that assumption meant that the staff had certain negative views about the church group supporting Mr. Brigham. It was no great task to discover that the local Mormon group was descended from those who had not completed the trek to Utah in the previous century, a group which, with minor exceptions, is indistinguishable from middle-of-the-road midwestern Protestantism. That discovery immediately removed the prevailing sense, in the staff's mind, of the alien character of the religious group that Mr. Brigham had joined.

When I talked with Mr. Brigham in the presence of the staff, the crucial part of the conversation turned out to be about the devil. When Mr. Brigham used the term I felt the staff wince. I was able to talk about the devil with Mr. Brigham, with the happy result that he said the temptations of the devil, as his church taught, were never so strong as to override his ability, with the help of God and the support of his fellows, to say no to them. This view seemed to me sound demonology admitting that the capacity for responsibility is qualified but not overturned. Both of us seemed to feel at home in that discussion and I endeavored, by approaching the topic from more than one angle, to help Mr. Brigham articulate his convictions and hence for him to become more secure in holding them. When we had finished, the staff was surprised at what had been revealed. Wisely, they did not rescind their judgment that Mr. Brigham was still unstable. But both Mr. Brigham's own ability to assume responsibility, and the teaching of his church group along with its support, appeared as more positive factors than they had before.

Mrs. Gowan was a married woman in her late forties without children. About two years previously Mrs. Gowan had been hospitalized for a rather severe depression. She had responded well to treatment and after some months had been able to return home although she continued to make periodic visits to the hospital. Some months before I saw her, she had been readmitted to the hospital on the advice of the staff and with the concurrence of Mrs. Gowan and her husband. At first she made considerable progress as she had on the first admission; thus she was permitted to return home to sleep and spend her mornings while she came back to the hospital each afternoon. Just before the consultation in which I was involved, that plan broke down. Mrs. Gowan was now back in the hospital full time. The antidepressive treatment had been applied but it was not working as in her first admission. The staff declared themselves at an impasse about what to do. On the one hand, Mrs. Gowan's disorientation was less than on her first admission; on the other hand, the measures that had helped her at first were clearly not now effective. The staff knew, they said, that Mrs. Gowan was a Catholic, but my questions showed that they had not explored what, in particular, her Catholic faith meant to her.

In my conversation with Mrs. Gowan, I discovered that although Mrs. Gowan was Catholic, her husband was not, and that she felt guilty before God because she had been unable to bring her husband into the faith. Also she had not been to mass or confession since well before her first hospital admission even though no barriers to such activity had been set by the staff and a priest was available in the hospital on call. When I asked her whether she would like to have us call the priest on her behalf, she was notably resistive.

After considerably more discussion than the above excerpt suggests, I formed the hypothesis that Mrs. Gowan was trying to carry out her own atonement. Perhaps the dynamics had been present though concealed during her first admission, but they had been obscured by the severely depressed condition and the successful application of antidepressive treatment. It seemed indeed the partial release that this treatment provided for her that brought into the open her self-atoning tendencies, and her failure to use just those resources that she claimed to believe in. I can recall that the staff, once they grasped the theological idea, remained after hours to explore its possible applicability to Mrs. Gowan, finally concluding that it gave them a new understanding and hence a new way of approaching Mrs. Gowan.

Since both these hospital cases are partial success stories, perhaps it is important to add that pastoral and theological diagnosis by no means invariably has such relatively happy outcomes.

The following situational illustrations took place in college and church settings.

A college chaplain was approached by a nineteen-year-old student, John Dark, who had transferred to this college after experiencing what he called considerable "anxiety" the previous year at a school in another part of the country. Soon after his arrival at this college, a fellow student had committed suicide which triggered John's fear that he might do the same thing. He told the chaplain he felt depressed, that his stomach was tied in knots, and added that he thought he might have some "spiritual difficulty."

A half dozen interviews were held, the principal result of which appeared to be increasing John's confidence in the chaplain. At that point the chaplain believed John ought to see a psychiatrist to check the nature of the depression, and decided the relationship had reached a point where such a recommendation could be made. John did see the part-time college psychiatrist who prescribed medication to help John cope with his feelings. The following day John sought out the chaplain again and, while indicating that he got help from the psychiatrist, expressed shock at the fact that the psychiatrist had been drinking a cocktail during their interview. The chaplain made a point not to comment on or to inquire further about the doctor's alleged drinking, saying only, "I'm glad you let me know about your disappointment."

On his own initiative the student then, for the first time, talked about his brother, indicating that his father, whom he described as like Archie Bunker, took the brother as his favorite but also picked on him more. The thread that led from drinking to brother and father was that the brother had begun to drink while John had not. After further discussion of brother and father, the following conversation ensued:

> John: You know, it seems that I feel closer to Satan often . . . than I do to God.
> Chaplain: God seems so far away and Satan seems so close? What does God want of you, do you think?
> John: My trust, and my confidence in him, and confidence in myself.
> Chaplain: Did you say that for my sake?
> John: I guess I did. Actually I don't think I even believe in God.

The discussion in religious language continued. The chaplain did indeed fail to follow up the Satan clue and peddled God instead. Nevertheless he was shrewd enough to recognize that he had done so, and the continuation of the discussion in religious terms including ending with a prayer does not appear to have been forced. At the close of this meeting, arrangements were made for another interview.

In his written analysis of the situation, the chaplain noted that he believed depressed persons usually need at least consultation with a psychiatrist, and indicated that he himself planned to ask the psychiatrist about John Dark, with the latter's permission. Whatever the reasons, however, he noted he appeared to have established a positive relationship with John that the psychiatrist was probably unable to duplicate, and thought he ought to try a little longer to mediate help.

In his theological analysis of the situation, the chaplain emphasized three points: First he suggested he could keep down his own fears about whether he was succeeding or not by relying on "the pastoral presence as a sign of God's care"; second, noting the mixed feelings about John's father, he suggested he might in some measure serve as a kind of intermediary to help John gain more appropriate capacity to trust; and third, he thought it probable that John wanted forgiveness especially in the light of his father's negative judgment.

In a written evaluation to the chaplain on his work and reflections, I noted, "Your ability to make a theological analysis of a situation has improved; but you have not entirely got rid of the notion that theology is what things ought to be and not first what they really are." I then tried to spell out that point to help the chaplain profit from it.

Another way I could have put my point was to state that the chaplain had tried to skip theological or pastoral diagnosis. Granted the paucity of data, I would tend to diagnose the situation somewhat as follows: John Dark probably suffers from a mild depression, no doubt originally triggered in relationships with his father and his brother. The depression seems to combine some guilt and some resentment. But the student is imaginative, and along with the depression he probably has also a certain amount of despair. He finds himself deterred from looking ahead by the chaotic nature of his feelings. Hence his establishing a relationship with someone not afraid to be in a fatherly role, who notes his despair and not just his depression or guilt or anger, may indeed be a sign of God's care he needed to have; and it may be useful to him if it is not just a refuge where he can hide.

From there I might use the chaplain's intuitions about the need for trust and forgiveness, but first I would put those matters in a diagnostic framework and try to think through how those things in the discussions of the chaplain and John could be made realities. I would also return to the discussion about Satan and God, as the chaplain did not do, to see what meaning might be there. I challenged the chaplain about his reluctance to take on the devil in his conversation with John. While the chaplain's basic insights were good and theology was meaningful to him, he did not understand the need for diagnosis. He moved too quickly to a kind of treatment by theology which made his analysis too diffused and less helpful than the insights themselves warranted.

Another pastor, this one in a local church, reported a situation that occurs frequently in pastoral experience. After a young people's meeting on Sunday evening, teenager Mary Jones talked with the pastor and told him that Christian faith was very meaningful to her. The next day the pastor decided to visit Mary at her home to continue their conversation. When he arrived Mary was on the telephone so he started to talk with Mary's mother. Mrs. Jones called in her husband and finally the pastor was engaged with father, mother, Mary, and Mary's sister. Mrs. Jones who was both intelligent and earnest about her religious faith did almost all the talking. She told the pastor she had attempted to get a small group of competent church people to attend meetings of the local school board but was unsuccessful. The only conversation the pastor had with Mary was a rather jerky set of suggestions about how Mary might attend a weekend work camp under church auspices.

In his appraisal of his call, the pastor expressed himself as pleased with the outcome because he had come to know the whole family, especially the mother, better. He indicated that he had intended to talk with Mary, but what actually had happened was perhaps more important. He offered no rationale for not following up Mrs. Jones's attempt to organize the church group, nor indeed any reason for his not requesting a chance to talk with Mary as he originally intended. There were no articulate theological reflections in his comments. Yet the situation was theologically intriguing. Under the mother's leadership, the family clearly regarded itself as positively Christian, and Mary had adopted something similar to her mother's concern. But what was the real nature of this interest? Was it a kind of pietism, even a holier-than-thou attitude? Or was Mrs. Jones's concern for the school board weighted in a social action direction? To diagnose the nature of the religious interest would have been the first step in this situation. The pastor, not seeing this opportunity, simply let it go by and patted himself on the back for having listened. Just this kind of work and reflection goes on far too often. Had there been an overt problem brought to the pastor, he would probably have done better by it. But it is in just such relatively routine situations that diagnosis may become more intriguing, yet familiarity may breed blindness to what one could find out.

Another pastor reported a series of interviews and home visits he made with a family in which the father, in his mid-thirties, was in a wheelchair suffering from a terminal illness, while the mother was tired of living with a sick partner who refused to let her do anything for him. At times each spouse would calm down enough to discuss possible constructive action with the pastor, but mostly emotions and tempers flared and names were called. The situation continued for months and no resolution was reached.

The minister in this situation attempted a genuinely pastoral diagnosis. He realized that his own temptation was to be moralistic, to condemn the wife because of her hostility to a husband who could not recover from his illness, and to try to make the husband into a passively grateful dying man. His analysis made considerable use of the concept of sin, showing how actual sin and original or collective sin were interwoven in each person and the relationship between them in such a fashion that what was elicited from him was not condemnation but understanding and compassion. He noted that the repression of the aggressive energies in either or both persons might well have been worse from a theological point of view. Even though the situation was difficult, and he never succeeded in making any significant change in it, his diagnosis nevertheless enabled him to continue his relationship with both persons without self-recrimination.

One of the most important diagnostic opportunities of the pastor is in dealing with people who do not say, "I have a problem. Help me solve it." Perhaps some day such a problem may arise in their lives. But whether at that point they would go to the pastor may well depend on the relationship he has built up in the interim. Such relationships offer diagnostic opportunities of a kind that psychiatrists seldom have.

I have presented excerpts from several specific situations in order to suggest the meaning of pastoral diagnosis in a normative sense. I believe it is just this method, exercised more systematically, that needs to be used to build up a more comprehensive understanding of pastoral diagnosis. I find myself reluctant to select from theological teachings illustrations that seem more useful for diagnostic purposes than others, for probably such a list would represent a bias either of myself personally or of my part of the theological tradition. Thus, theory building about diagnosis should perhaps be coterminous with all theological concepts believed to be significant, rather than with a few. But if they are to be used diagnostically as relevant, the pastor must have mastery of them, and not be tied to certain forms or languages in which they have appeared.

The brevity of my cases has not permitted me to show sufficiently the process of diagnosis in which the other person participates creatively. And yet in spite of the necessary sketchiness of these accounts, I hope I have clarified that pastoral diagnosis must consider kinds of situations rarely encountered by psychiatry, that theological understandings can illuminate situations including the pastor's own part in them, that dynamic insights may be used without adopting the framework of other professions, and that pastoral diagnosis is a process and not a single event.

References

CLEBSCH, W. A. & JAEKLE, C. R.: *Pastoral Care in Historical Perspective.* Englewood Cliffs, NJ: Prentice-Hall, 1964.
HILTNER, SEWARD: *Religion and Health.* New York: Macmillan, 1943.
————: *Pastoral Counseling.* Nashville: Abingdon Press, 1949.
————: *Theological Dynamics.* Nashville: Abingdon Press, 1972.
McNEILL, J. T.: *A History of the Cure of Souls.* New York: Harper & Row, 1951.
McNEILL, J. T. & GAMER, H. M.: *Medieval Handbooks of Penance.* New York: Columbia University Press, 1938.
MENNINGER, KARL et al.: *The Vital Balance.* New York: Viking Press, 1963.
SPENCER, ICHABOD: *A Pastor's Sketches.* New York: Dodd, Mead & Co., 1853.

TOWARD AUTONOMOUS SOCIAL DIAGNOSIS

SCOTT BRIAR, D.S.W.*

My thinking about diagnosis has been profoundly and permanently affected by a paper on the theory of diagnosis by D. Ewen Cameron (1953). In that paper he says, ". . . the diagnosis made in any society will be greatly affected by the basic premises existing in that society concerning power . . ." (p. 34). By "power" Cameron means ". . . the force which brings things about; for instance, the power which makes the crops grow, the power which causes accidents, the power which gives one man authority over others" (pp. 34–35). Cameron argues that diagnosis should be a "design for action" as opposed to diagnosis merely as classification, on the one hand, or as a search for the causes and dynamics of a problem, on the other. Cameron's implication is that the only function of diagnosis is to assist in designing effective treatment; diagnostic efforts directed toward other questions or purposes are of dubious value to the practitioner.

Over the years I have found Cameron's view that diagnosis should provide direct guidelines for treatment planning accepted without question by many clinicians. However, in spite of the seemingly widespread agreement that diagnosis should serve as a design for action, I have spent countless hours attending diagnostic conferences in which lengthy and extensive discussions of the possible causes and dynamics of patients' problems led to designs for action no

---

* Dean, School of Social Work, University of Washington, Seattle, Washington.

more specific than the conclusion that further treatment was indicated. While I think it is intrinsically important and inherently interesting to try to explain or understand why something happened or why someone behaves as he does, such explanations, even if they can be achieved, are often of no direct use in planning effective intervention. In other words, knowledge about the cause of a problem or condition rarely tells us what to do about it. For example, it has been suggested that the Industrial Revolution is a principal cause of some of our current social problems. Even if that is true, and it may well be, it does not tell us what to do about these problems since we can neither stop the Industrial Revolution nor return to the world as it was.

Cameron's point is that the diagnostic conceptions we use are related to our assumptions about power, that is, our assumptions about what makes things happen and especially what we believe we can do to make things happen. Thus, if clinicians believe, correctly or incorrectly, that discovering the causes of patients' problems will increase their chances of helping these patients, then clinicians naturally will devote attention to a search for causes. The influence of clinicians' assumptions on their diagnostic judgments has been demonstrated in a number of studies of clinical judgment reported by Bieri et al. (1966). For example, some studies indicate that clinicians prefer some diagnostic categories over others and ascribe their preferred diagnoses to those patients with whom they would most like to work and with whom they believe they are most likely to be successful. Other studies show that diagnostic judgments vary if the patient's socioeconomic characteristics are varied, even though all other information about the patient is held constant. Clinicians apparently vary their diagnoses because they believe certain social characteristics have differential prognostic probabilities associated with them.

What form should the diagnostic process take if clinicians are to give more than lip service to the idea that diagnostic activity must be relevant to treatment, that it must lead to a design for action? Cameron implies that diagnostic categories should be constructed neither a priori nor on etiological premises but rather ought to be constructed according to differential responses of patients to specific interventions. In other words, the important diagnostic question is which persons and problems respond to a particular treatment. The answer should be derived from the empirical differences found between those who have and have not responded favorably to the treatment. This approach has yet to be followed to any considerable extent; however, some efforts in this direction can be found in recent research on the diagnosis of schizophrenia and in behavioral therapy (NIMH Research Task Force 1975).

I shall begin to develop the theme of diagnosis as a design for action in relation to social diagnosis by making some observations about the field's background and current status. Adolf Meyer (1951) was one of the first to give systematic attention to the significance of social and cultural factors in psychiatric diagnosis; however, the importance of these factors in mental illness had been recognized earlier —one of the reasons social workers were brought into the mental health field. Traditionally, the social history—information about the patient's family and social origins—was regarded as useful if only supplementary information in arriving at a differential diagnosis of the patient's psychiatric condition. Information about the patient's current social situation was typically used the same way. For example, information that the patient had recently become unemployed was viewed as a sign of added stress which might have exacerbated or perpetuated the patient's condition. By the same token, intervention in the patient's social environment was seen as supplementary to treatment, not as a primary form of treatment in itself. Working with the patient's family or improving the patient's social situation was done only to make it possible for the primary treatment effort to proceed more effectively. To summarize: (1) In traditional psychiatric practice, the patient's social situation was viewed as contributing to the patient's problem, but rarely was seen as the problem itself; and (2) while social intervention might support psychiatric treatment, it was not considered a primary form of treatment.

This perspective became increasingly untenable as mounting evidence indicated that social factors can be primary and central in mental illness and that social intervention sometimes can be more potent than psychotherapeutic treatment in alleviating some psychiatric problems. One example of this changing perspective is the development of family therapy which emerged after some clinicians began to suggest not only that the patient's pathology was a manifestation of pathology in the patient's family but also that the patient's condition would not improve unless intervention were directed at the family—a fundamental departure from the previous view that the family's contribution was to the genesis of the patient's disorder. In fact, some present-day advocates of family therapy have even gone so far as to claim that *all* mental health problems are essentially family problems and that all treatment therefore should be family oriented; however, this assertion is just as absurd as saying that *none* of the problems patients bring are family problems. The difficulty is that we do not yet know how to discriminate in a reliable, valid way between family and nonfamily problems or how to identify those cases in which family treatment would be the most effective form of intervention. One reason for this uncertainty is the unfortunate lack of research on the effectiveness of family therapy. Moreover, of the few studies that have been done, some appear to have been ignored by practitioners. For example, multiple impact therapy (MacGregor et al. 1964), one relatively successful approach to family therapy, is no longer being used, except on a small scale in a few isolated places.

An important point to remember is that families themselves live in a social environment which means that some of the problems families present may be manifestations of developments in the family's social environment (S. Briar 1964). A good example is the impact of unemployment on families and individuals (K. Briar 1976). Families subjected to sudden, unexpected unemployment tend to experience similar response patterns. At certain stages following the onset of unemployment, many families begin to exhibit several signs of disturbance, namely: (1) increased interpersonal conflict within the family (between husband and wife, between parents and children, and among siblings); (2) deterioration of long established family patterns and structures; and (3) manifestations of depression—sometimes severe—in individual family members. In other words, the behavior of these families could be diagnosed as manifestations of family pathology and emotional disorder. Such diagnoses could lead to the conclusion that these problems should be treated with family therapy, individual psychotherapy, or perhaps other forms of psychiatric treatment—an approach that has been followed in some programs established to help the unemployed.

An alternative would be to recognize these disturbed behavior patterns as responses to a social problem for which social intervention—in this case, providing employment—may be appropriate. The probable efficacy of such an approach is suggested by the marked improvement in the functioning of those families in which the breadwinner is able to find employment before the family's deterioration becomes solidified. In the United States, a social program—unemployment compensation—was established to mitigate the problem of unemployment; however, this program is grossly inadequate. Unemployment assaults individuals and families in two principal ways: First, this society attaches a severe stigma to those who do not work, expecting all except the very young, the old, the sick, and the disabled to work. Second, unemployment typically means a cessation of income, thus destroying the family's source of necessary material support. However, the present unemployment compensation program in the United States (1) does not create jobs, (2) does not provide a level of financial support at the income level needed by most if not all families receiving it, and (3) does not cover all of the unemployed. A more far-reaching, effective social program would not only directly improve the mental health of those who are unemployed and their families but also would prevent a much larger number of individuals and families from experiencing the same problems.

Few practitioners who encounter families manifesting these symptoms of unemployment consider themselves in a position to create jobs for their clients. In that regard, the example of unemployment illustrates another problem in social diagnosis and social intervention. When personal or family disorders are diagnosed as manifestations of social problems, the diagnosis often seems to imply a need for social interventions requiring social changes of a magnitude beyond the capacity of most or perhaps all practitioners. In other words, creating jobs on a large scale is not easy and establishing a program to accomplish that goal would be difficult. By contrast, if the problem is diagnosed as psychological, emotional, or interpersonal, the clinician is likely to believe it is at least within his capacity to deal with it. I do not mean to say that the clinician will be effective or successful, but only that to the clinician the task does not seem to be inherently beyond his capacity. That, you will recall, was Cameron's point: Practitioners' conceptions of diagnosis are related to their assumptions about power, especially their own capacity to make things happen. And that, I suggest, is one of the reasons why there has been a strong preference for psychological rather than social diagnosis and intervention—namely, we believe we have a greater capacity to bring about psychological change. That assumption needs to be challenged in light of the discouraging results of the research on the effectiveness of traditional psychotherapy as compared to approaches that rely on modifications of the environment.

There is a more general point here: If diagnosis is a plan for action, then social diagnosis is likely to become increasingly autonomous as the theory and technology of social intervention develop. As this development proceeds, we will be faced increasingly with the problem of differential social and psychological diagnosis and intervention. An earlier example of this sort of choice was the debate in the late 1950s and early 1960s about how to combat racism: Some argued for attitude change through education as the only effective approach; others favored direct social intervention through court action and legislation. In view of subsequent events, few would disagree that in this case social intervention was the more effective approach.

However, the distinction between social and psychological should not be overemphasized. Such distinctions are more arbitrary than real and were invented to facilitate analysis. Persons and their behaviors come in wholes and we take them apart in the hope of increasing our understanding of them. Basically, we are trying to make a distinction between exogenous and endogenous influences and interventions. While that distinction is far from clean and while many important things appear to happen at the interface between the two, the distinction still seems to have some heuristic value. My point is that if a theory and technology of social intervention—and therefore of social diagnosis—are to be developed, we will need to have some sense of what is and what is not a social intervention.

To facilitate this task, I shall suggest some beginning definitions. Social interventions consist of deliberate alterations in conditions and contingencies in the social environment. Such interventions can occur either at the "micro" level where alterations are made to help an individual person or family or at the "macro" level where alterations are made to affect groups of persons or families. Therefore, the task of social diagnosis would be to determine which conditions or contingencies should be altered and to what ends or objectives.

"Macro" social interventions have become increasingly significant in modern societies. Despite widespread dissatisfaction with some of these social programs, they are likely not only to continue but to increase in the future. Yet, in spite of all the effort and resources invested in large-scale social interventions, we still know remarkably little about how to predict what the effects of new social interventions will be or even how to make sure that a new social program is implemented in the way it was intended to be. The technology of "macro" social intervention still is unfortunately rather primitive.

Practitioners in the human services have long been engaged in "micro" social intervention. On a case by case basis, clinicians have made attempts to improve the client's condition by making alterations in the client's social environment. However, such social interventions, which loom large in the work of many practitioners, have received little attention and almost no systematic study, in contrast, for example, to the rather substantial amount of research devoted to psychological interventions in counseling and psychotherapy. This neglect is unfortunate since the anecdotal reports of many practitioners indicate that "micro" social intervention can have a profound and dramatic effect on the patient's behavior.

Because those of us who work in the mental health field recognize that social conditions and contingencies can have profound adverse effects on persons and families, it is remarkable that we have not given more attention to the systematic exploration of social intervention as a means of promoting positive mental health. There are exceptions. Milieu therapy is one, although the potential inherent in that movement has not yet been fully realized (Price et al. 1974). Another exception is behavior therapy. Much of behavior therapy consists of the systematic alteration of conditions and contingencies in the social environment, e.g., the creation and use of token economies in psychiatric hospitals. The work of behavioral therapists—if we can set aside for a moment the polemics that have surrounded that movement—is also important in illustrating the kind of precise and detailed analysis that would be necessary to build an adequate theory and technology of social intervention.

To develop a theory and technology of social intervention and thereby a foundation for social diagnosis, research must proceed. We need more studies, especially clinical studies, of the effects of both "micro" and "macro" social interventions on the lives of individual persons and families. In addition, we need direct clinical experimentation with social intervention. For example, two of my students conducted a clinical experiment on a hospital ward in which they attempted to determine whether some modest social interventions (they compared several) could increase the percentage of discharged patients who returned for follow-up examination and treatment. The base line rate of return was about fifty percent, and they were able to improve that figure. Such an experiment, which may at first seem trivial, assumes greater importance in view of the recognized significance of utilization behavior among patients in the cost and effectiveness of health care. More generally, we need to make rather wide-ranging efforts to learn more about the conditions under which social interventions are effective.

We also need to do something often discussed but rarely done, namely, to delve more deeply into the experiences of those who have successfully recovered from severe problems and disturbances. We know, for example, that social conditions can determine whether a discharged psychiatric patient will be rehospitalized, but we have not followed that insight with detailed studies of the social situations of those patients who remained out of the hospital and who were functioning successfully. Similar studies with ex-convicts who do not recidivate, with former delinquents who do not become adult criminals, and with successful adults who grew up in adverse circumstances might provide more specific understanding of the role that social conditions and contingencies play in promoting positive mental health.

Would the results of such endeavors be worth the effort? Mental health practitioners know how incredibly powerful the social environment can be in its adverse effects on the well-being of persons. It can be equally powerful in a positive direction. However, the positive influence of the social environment is less obvious because the belief system of our culture allows us to blame the environment for our failures but encourages us to take personal, autonomous credit for our successes. What I am proposing and what the notion of autonomous social diagnosis implies is that we need to learn not only how to recognize and decrease the social environment's negative effects but, even more important, how to marshall and shape the powerful positive influences that the social environment can and does have on the quality of life.

References

BIERI, JAMES et al.: *Social and Clinical Judgment: The Discrimination of Behavioral Information.* New York: Wiley, 1966.

BRIAR, KATHARINE: The Effects of Long-Term Unemployment on Workers and Their Families. Doctoral Dissertation, University of California at Berkeley, Berkeley, California, 1976 (unpublished).

BRIAR, SCOTT: The Family as an Organization: An Approach to Family Diagnosis and Treatment. *Soc. Service Rev.* 38(3):247–55, 1964.

CAMERON, D. E.: A Theory of Diagnosis. In *Current Problems in Psychiatric Diagnosis*, P. H. Hoch & Joseph Zubin, eds., pp. 33–45. New York: Grune & Stratton, 1953.

MacGREGOR, ROBERT et al.: *Multiple Impact Therapy with Families.* New York: McGraw-Hill, 1964.

MEYER, ADOLF: *Collected Papers of Adolf Meyer*, Vol. 3, E. E. Winters, ed. Baltimore: Johns Hopkins Press, 1951.

NIMH RESEARCH TASK FORCE: *Research in the Service of Mental Health: Report of the Research Task Force of the National Institute of Mental Health.* DHEW Publication No. ADM 75-236, 1975.

PRICE, RILEY et al.: Behavior Modification in Total Institutions. In *Successful Group Care*, Martin Wolins, ed., pp. 365–90. Chicago: Aldine, 1974.

EPILOGUE

What needs to be said in concluding this conference is that diagnosing, for all the painstaking attention that has been paid to it in this series of presentations, is not an end in itself.

Diagnosing is in the service of caring—it is indeed a form of caring in a posture of serving. It is, therefore, fitting to end on a note taken from a great caring person, a great servant, a great intellectual, and a great physician, who extended his care to individuals while also being a shrewd diagnostician of his civilization. That man is Albert Schweitzer, from whose *Reverence for Life* these passages come:

> The world does not consist of happenings only; it contains life as well, and to the life in the world, so far as it comes within my reach, I have to be in a relation which is not only passive but active. By placing myself in the service of that which lives, I reach an activity, exerted upon the world, which has meaning and purpose . . . . As a being in an active relation to the world one comes into a spiritual relation with it by not living for himself alone, but feeling himself one with all life that comes within his reach. He will feel all that life's experiences as his own, he will give it all the help that he possibly can, and will feel all the saving and promotion of life that he has been able to effect as the deepest happiness that can ever fall to his lot.

These words are not a bad motto for the Menninger Foundation's next fifty years.

P.W.P.

INDEX

207